# Oracle Certification Prep

## Study Guide for

## 1Z0-060: Upgrade to Oracle Database 12c

Matthew Morris

**Study Guide for Upgrade to Oracle Database 12c
(Exam 1Z0-060) Rev 1.0**

ISBN-13: 978-1-941404-02-7
ISBN-10: 1941404022

# Table of Contents

What to expect from the test ................................................... 10

What to Expect from this Study Guide .................................... 11

Additional Study Resources .................................................... 12

Enterprise Manager and Other Tools ..................................... 13

Use EM Express.................................................................... 13

Use OUI, DBCA for installation and configuration ................... 17

Basics of Multitenant Container Database (CDB) ..................... 30

Identify the benefits of the multitenant container database ............... 30

Explain root and multitenant architecture ............................ 31

Configuring and Creating CDBs and PDBs .............................. 33

Create and configure a CDB ................................................ 33

Create and configure a PDB ................................................ 36

Migrate a non-CDB to a PDB database ................................. 41

Managing CDBs and PDBs ..................................................... 43

Establish connection to a CDB/PDB ..................................... 43

Start up and shut down a CDB/PDB..................................... 45

Change instance parameters for a CDB/PDB ......................... 49

Managing Tablespaces, Common and Local Users, Privileges and Roles ..50

Manage tablespaces in a CDB/PDB....................................... 50

Manage users and privileges for CDB/PDB ........................... 51

Backup, Recovery and Flashback for a CDB/PDB ..................... 56

Perform backup of CDB and PDB ......................................... 56

Perform recovery of CDB and PDB....................................... 57

Perform Flashback for a CDB ................................................. 61

Information Lifecycle Management and Storage Enhancements ............. 62

Use ILM features ............................................................ 62

Perform tracking and automated data placement ........................ 63

Move a datafile online ..................................................... 66

In-Database Archiving and Valid-Time Temporal ........................... 67

Differentiate between ILM and Valid-Time Temporal ................... 67

Set and use Valid Time Temporal ......................................... 67

Use In-Database archiving .................................................. 71

Auditing ....................................................................... 73

Enable and configure Unified Audit Data Trail ......................... 73

Create and enable audit policies .......................................... 77

Privileges ..................................................................... 81

Use administrative privileges .............................................. 81

Create, enable and use privilege analysis ............................... 82

Oracle Data Redaction ....................................................... 85

Use and manage Oracle Data Redaction policies ....................... 85

RMAN and Flashback Data Archive ........................................... 91

Use RMAN enhancements .................................................... 91

Implement the new features in Flashback Data Archive ............... 94

Real-Time Database Operation Monitoring ................................. 95

Implement real-time database operation monitoring ................... 95

SQL Tuning .................................................................... 99

Use Adaptive Execution Plans ............................................. 99

Use enhanced features of statistics gathering ......................... 102

Use Adaptive SQL Plan Management ..................................... 105

Emergency Monitoring, Real-Time ADDM, Compare Period ADDM, and Active Session History (ASH) Analytics.....................................................108

Perform emergency monitoring and real-time ADDM .......................108

Generate ADDM Compare Period.......................................................110

Diagnose performance issues using ASH enhancements ...................112

Resource Manager and Other Performance Enhancements .................115

Use Resource Manager for a CDB and PDB .........................................115

Explain Multi-process Multi-threaded Oracle architecture ...............116

Use Flash Cache ................................................................................117

Index and Table Enhancements..........................................................119

Use Index enhancements..................................................................119

Use Table enhancements..................................................................119

Use Online operation enhancements ...............................................120

ADR and Network Enhancements.......................................................122

Explain ADR enhancements ..............................................................122

Oracle Data Pump, SQL*Loader, External Tables and Online Operations Enhancements .................................................................................124

Use Oracle Data Pump enhancements ..............................................124

Use SQL*Loader and External table enhancements...........................127

Partitioning Enhancements................................................................130

Explain Partitioning enhancements ..................................................130

Explain Index enhancements for partitioned tables..........................134

SQL Enhancements ...........................................................................137

Use Oracle Database Migration Assistant for Unicode.......................137

Use Row limiting clause, and secure file LOBs enhancements ...........138

Configure extended data types..........................................................141

Core Administration..........................................................................142

Explain the fundamentals of DB architecture ...................................142

Install and configure a database ....................................................146

Configure server and client network for a database ...........................146

Monitor database alerts ...............................................................152

Perform daily administration tasks .................................................155

Apply and review patches ............................................................156

Back up and recover the database...................................................161

Troubleshoot network and database issues .....................................170

Detect and repair data failures with Data Recovery Advisor...............173

Implement Flashback Technology ...................................................177

Load and Unload Data ..................................................................186

Relocate SYSAUX occupants ..........................................................195

Create a default permanent tablespace ...........................................196

Use the Redo Logfile Size Advisor...................................................197

Use Secure File LOBs....................................................................197

Use Direct NFS ...........................................................................199

Performance Management..............................................................201

Design the database layout for optimal performance..........................201

Monitor performance ...................................................................202

Manage memory..........................................................................204

Analyze and identify performance issues .........................................208

Perform real application testing .....................................................211

Use Resource Manager to manage resources ....................................216

Implement Application Tuning .......................................................219

Storage......................................................................................221

Manage database structures ..........................................................221

Administer ASM ........................................................................225

Manage ASM disks and diskgroups.......................................229

Manage ASM instance ...........................................................233

Manage VLDB..........................................................................236

Implement Space Management..............................................238

Security .......................................................................................244

Develop and implement a security policy............................244

Configure and manage auditing............................................246

Create the password file .......................................................248

Implement column and tablespace encryption ...................250

Performing Post-Upgrade Tasks ...............................................254

Migrate to unified auditing....................................................254

Perform post-upgrade tasks ..................................................255

Migrating Data by Using Oracle Data Pump .............................257

Migrate data by using Oracle Data Pump .............................257

# What to expect from the test

This test is broken into two sections, with each scored separately. You must pass both sections in order to be granted the certification. The first section is on the 12c new features. It contains 51 questions and requires a score of 64% to pass. The second section on Core DBA skills contains 34 questions and requires a score of 65% to pass. The questions will be either multiple choice or multiple answer and you will have 120 minutes to take the whole exam.

Ninety-four questions in a two-hour timeframe provides a bit under 77 seconds per question. This is a bit under the average, so this exam may cause you to have a time crunch. On exams where time may be a particular concern, I normally try to look at the clock only as I answer questions that mark the first three quarters of the exam (23, 47, and 70 for this exam) and compare with the time remaining. With a two-hour test, if I hit those questions at or below 30, 60, and 90 minutes respectively, then I am on track to complete the test on time. Do not constantly spend time watching the clock. That will serve no purpose, waste seconds and make you nervous besides.

When you sit to take the exam for 1Z0-060, you must understand what has been added or changed in the database with 12c, how that change affects using or administering the database, and the steps required to enable, disable, or configure the new feature. You won't be programming PL/SQL statements or navigating a GUI interface during the test.

The second portion of the exam is all about the common tasks performed by database administrators. If you have been working as a DBA, this section may be a walk in the park. If you have never worked as a DBA, have not done so recently, or have not used the specific features being tested, be sure to spend extra time preparing for the topics you are least comfortable with. I suspect more people will fail the exam from the Core DBA skills than the new features.

# What to Expect from this Study Guide

This study guide will cover the majority of changes that were made to the Oracle database between the Oracle 11g and 12c releases and provide a refresher on the Core DBA skills that have been listed as topics for this exam. While the topics provided by Oracle University for the new features were fairly specific, several topics provided for the Core DBA skills are extremely vague. An example of one of the broader topics is "Perform Daily Administration Tasks". The potential range of questions that could fit in this topic is enormous. The expectation from OU for this exam is that the people taking it have worked as Oracle database administrators and will know much of this information because they have done it. If you have not worked with the database, plan to spend a good bit of time preparing with multiple sources to become familiar with administration tasks.

This guide assumes that you are already have a reasonable level of familiarity with Oracle. Both the test and the guide are targeted for individuals who are already Oracle Certified Professional DBAs. You should have already taken and passed several exams demonstrating that you have knowledge of the Oracle database. This book is intended as much as possible to present information that is likely to be on the test at the <u>level</u> it will be presented on the test. As an example, for your career as an Oracle DBA, it would be ideal if you knew all of the PL/SQL procedures required to perform create an Oracle Resource Manager plan and could type them in without referring to the documentation. For the test, however, what is likely to be asked is the type of action that would be performed by Resource Manager for a given situation.

When studying for any certification test, you should utilize multiple resources. The companion website for this series has links to all of the relevant Oracle manuals plus links to white papers and articles that I found useful while researching this book. The guide will serve to focus you on the information most likely to be asked. The material at the website will help to provide additional context for that information. Preparing using both sets of data should help prevent you from missing key facts that will be needed on the test.

# Additional Study Resources

The companion website to this series is www.oraclecertificationprep.com. The site contains many additional resources that can be used to study for this exam (and others). From the entry page of the website, click on the 'Exams' button, and then select the link for this test. The Exam Details page contains links to the following information sources:

- Applicable Oracle documentation.
- Third-party books relevant to the exam.
- White papers and articles on Oracle Learning Library on topics covered in the exam.
- Articles on the Web that may be useful for the exam.

The website will <u>never</u> link to unauthorized content such as brain dumps or illegal content such as copyrighted material made available without the consent of the author. I cannot guarantee the accuracy of the content links. While I have located the data and scanned it to ensure that it is relevant to the given exam, I did not write it and have not proofread it from a technical standpoint. The material on the Oracle Learning Library is almost certain to be completely accurate and most of the other links come from highly popular Oracle support websites and are created by experienced Oracle professionals.

I recommend that you use more than one source of study materials whenever you are preparing for a certification. Reading information presented from multiple different viewpoints can help to give you a more complete picture of any given topic. The links on the website can help you to do this. Fully understanding the information covered in this certification is not just valuable so that getting a passing score is more likely – it will also help you in your career. I guarantee that in the long run, any knowledge you gain while studying for this certification will provide more benefit to you than any piece of paper or line on your resume.

# New Features of Oracle Database 12c

## Enterprise Manager and Other Tools

### Use EM Express

The EM Express utility is a web-based interface that allows you to manage the Oracle database from a graphical user environment. The utility is built into the Oracle database and allows you to monitor and manage performance of the database and do perform some of the most common administration functions. From the web interface, you can view, create, and alter the various storage structures of the database. When you first log into EM Express, you will be presented with a page similar to the below:

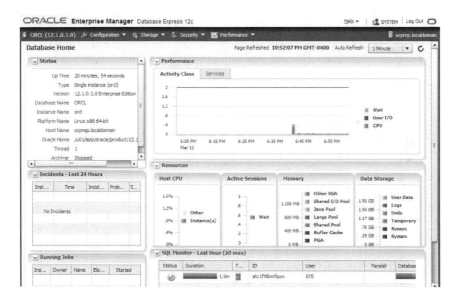

EM Express is specifically designed to be a lightweight interface that imposes negligible overhead on the database server itself. There are no background processes or tasks associated with the utility. It operates using only internal infrastructure components of the Oracle database, such as such as XDB and SQL*Net and utilizes data that is collected by existing Oracle database processes. EM Express data requests to the server are triggered when the user interacts with the web interface. The requested information is processed within the browser to minimize the load against the database server. Because it makes use of the database for its functionality, EM Express cannot perform actions outside the database. In addition, because EM Express makes use of Shockwave Flash (SWF) files, the web browser used must have the Flash plug-in installed.

Immediately upon logging in, you will be at the home page of EM Express. This page displays an overall view of the database instance status and activity. The administrative tasks available via EM Express can be accessed via four menus at the top of the page:

- **Configuration** -- The EM Express Configuration menu allows you to administer initialization parameters for one or more instances of the database. It displays the current memory configuration and the top processes consuming memory within the database. Administrators can also determine the usage of database features and database properties.
- **Storage** -- The storage administration functions allow DBAs to manage redo logs, archive logs, and tablespaces. It allows access to the Undo Advisor and undo statistics. EM Express also displays information regarding the contents of the control file.
- **Security** -- The security menu of EM Express allows DBAs to create and alter users, roles, and profiles as well as granting and revoking privileges.
- **Performance** -- The Performance Hub of EM Express displays performance data for a given time period. The information shown includes SQL Monitor, ASH Analytics, and ADDM. The hub also includes metrics that describe workload characteristics and database resource usage.


EM Express can be accessed via the EM Express URL provided by DBCA during the database configuration process. If you do not know which port EM Express was set to (the default is 5500), it is possible to determine the port with the following SQL statement:

```
SELECT DBMS_XDB_CONFIG.GETHTTPSPORT() FROM dual;
```

The EM Express URL will be in the following format:

```
https://database-hostname:portnumber/em/
```

For example:

```
https://dbhost.company.com:5500/em/
```

If the database instance is running, then the EM Express Login page should appear. If it is not running, you must start the instance prior to accessing EM Express. Provide the credentials of a user account that is authorized to access EM Express. A user that has been granted either the EM_EXPRESS_BASIC or EM_EXPRESS_ALL roles can log in to EM Express. Initially, that user could be either SYS or SYSTEM. However, using the SYS account is highly discouraged and it is recommended that you create a named user account for administering the database in lieu of the SYSTEM account.

### Configuring the HTTPS Port for EM Express

The port on which EM Express is accessed can be set or changed at need. Each database instance on a given host must use a unique port. If a port has not been configured for an instance, it is not possible to access EM Express. The steps to manually configure the port follow:

1. The Oracle Net Listener must have already been configured and started before a port can be set. The lsnrctl utility is used to start, stop, and view the status of the listener.

2. If the listener is not running on the default port of 1521, the init.ora file for the database to be managed with EM Express must contain a local_listener entry. The local_listener entry references a TNSNAMES

entry that points to the correct listener. For example, the entry local_listener=orcl1 would be required for an instance defined in the TNSNAMES.ORA file with a non-standard port of 1522 as follows:

```
orcl1= (DESCRIPTION=
        (ADDRESS=
         (PROTOCOL=tcp)(HOST=host_name)(PORT=1522)
        )
        (CONNECT_DATA=
         (SERVICE_NAME=service_name)(SERVER=DEDICATED)
        )
       )
```

3. The TCP dispatcher must be enabled by adding the following entry to the init.ora file for the database you want to manage using EM Express:

```
dispatchers="(PROTOCOL=TCP)(SERVICE=<sid>XDB)"
```

4. The database must be restarted in order for the changes made in the init.ora file to take effect.

5. The PL/SQL procedure DBMS_XDB_CONFIG.SETHTTPSPORT can then be used to set the HTTPS port for EM Express. This procedure will change the HTTPS port in the xdbconfig.xml file in the Oracle XML DB Repository. You must be connected with SYSDBA privileges in order to run the procedure. The following example sets the port to 5600:

```
exec DBMS_XDB_CONFIG.SETHTTPSPORT(5600);
```

The Oracle Database 2 Day DBA documentation for 12c covers the EM Express interface in greater detail. Ideally, you should install Oracle 12c and become familiar with the utility by accessing the various screens.

## Use OUI, DBCA for installation and configuration

The installation of the Oracle Database is a reasonably involved process and until you have done it a few times, the best bet is to have the installation manual for the proper OS open in your browser and to follow it step-by-step as you work. This chapter will cover some of the highlights of installing Oracle 12c on Oracle Linux 6. Before making any changes to the destination system, first check to ensure it meets the minimum requirements for installing Oracle 12c:

The disk space requirements for the software files (*not* the database files) on Linux x86-64 are:

- Enterprise Edition: 6.4 GB
- Standard Edition: 6.1 GB
- Standard Edition One: 6.1 GB


The memory requirements for installing Oracle Database 12c under Linux is 1 GB but 2 or more GB is recommended. The amount of swap space recommended depends on the amount or RAM in the system.

- For systems with 1-2 GB of ram, swap space should be 150% of the RAM.
- For systems with 2-16 GB of ram, swap space should be equal to the RAM.
- For systems with >16 GB of ram, swap space should be 16GB.


Once it has been determined that a system can host Oracle 12c, there are a number of pre-installation tasks that must be performed on a Linux server before running the Oracle installer. The complete list is in the Oracle installation manual for Linux. However, if you are running Oracle Linux 6, there is an Oracle RDBMS Server pre-install RPM package available. This package makes it <u>much</u> easier to install the Oracle Database. The pre-install RPM will perform most of the pre-install configuration tasks automatically. Among other things, the package creates the 'oracle' user and the groups needed for Oracle Database installation. It also modifies kernel parameters in /etc/sysctl.conf and resource limits in /etc/security/limits.conf. It ensures that several packages required by Oracle are installed on the system. This significantly reduces the amount of time required to prepare the server before installing the Oracle software. The following command will install the 12c pre-installer and prepare your OL6 system for the Oracle install:

```
yum install oracle-rdbms-server-12cR1-preinstall
```

Download the installation files from Oracle. For 64-bit Linux, there are two files, linuxamd64_12c_database_1of2 and linuxamd64_12c_database_2of2. These should be placed into the /tmp directory of your Linux server and then extracted in place as the oracle user with the unzip command:

```
[oracle@ocp tmp]unzip linuxamd64_12c_database_1of2.zip
. . .
[oracle@ocp tmp]unzip linuxamd64_12c_database_2of2.zip
. . .
```

Once the files are unzipped, change to the /tmp/database directory and run the Oracle installer:

```
[oracle@ocp database] ./runInstaller
```

If everything has been configured correctly, executing the installer should get you to the 'Configure Security Updates' screen of the Oracle 12c installation.

**Step 1: Configure Security Updates** -- In this screen, you will provide an email address where Oracle can inform you of security issues with the database. Optionally, you can opt to receive security updates via My Oracle Support.

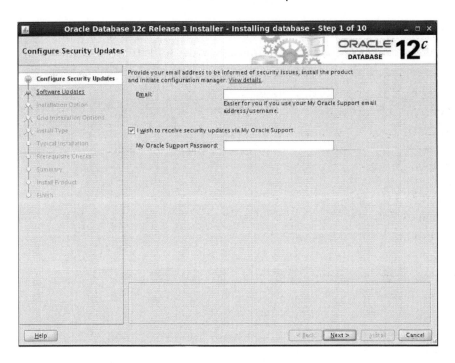

**Step 2: Download Software Updates** -- You can opt to download software updates via My Oracle Support if you have an account. Optionally, you can choose to use pre-downloaded updates or skip the software updates entirely.

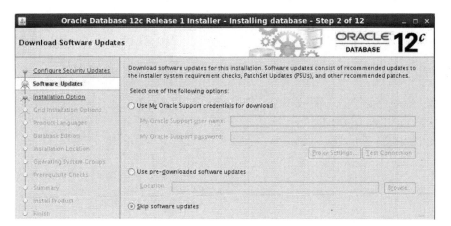

**Step 3: Installation Option** -- In this step you can choose to install the Oracle software and create a database, just install the software, or upgrade an existing software installation.

**Step 4: Grid Installation Options** -- This screen allows you to select between a single instance database installation, Oracle Real Application Clusters database installation, or Oracle RAC One Node database installation.

**Step 5: Product Language** -- In this screen you can add additional languages to the Oracle database installation.

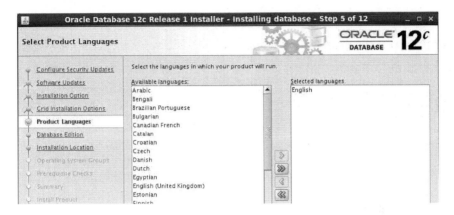

**Step 6: Database Edition** -- In this screen, you must select between installation the Oracle Enterprise, Standard Edition, or Standard Edition One product versions.

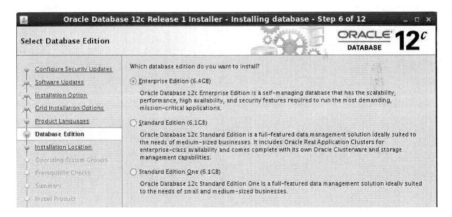

**Step 7: Installation Location** -- You can alter the default installation location of the software from this screen.

**Step 8: Create Inventory** -- This screen determines the locations to store the installation metadata files.

**Step 9: Operating System Groups** -- In this screen, operating system groups are mapped to database privileges.

**Step 10: Prerequisite Checks** -- The installer verifies that all of the prerequisites for an Oracle installation have been met. If any checks fail, they are listed in the screen. In this case, the swap space on the system is slightly below the expected value. I have clicked to ignore the warning and move on with the install.

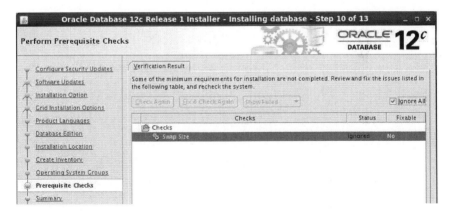

**Step 11: Summary** -- The installer displays a summary of the options chosen to this point in the install. You can choose to edit many of them from this screen.

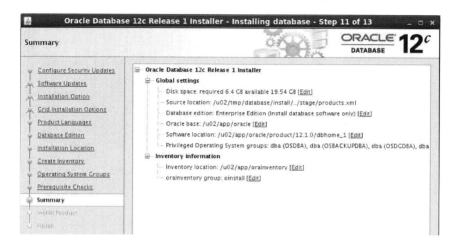

**Step 12: Install Product** -- In this screen, the installer performs the file copy and other installation tasks.

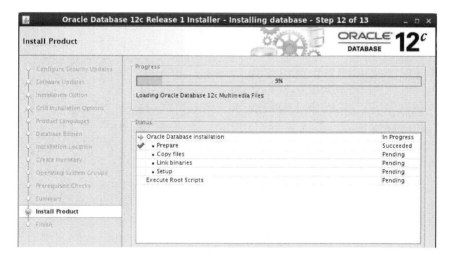

**Step 12a: Root Scripts** -- The final step of the installation requires two
scripts to be run as the root user.

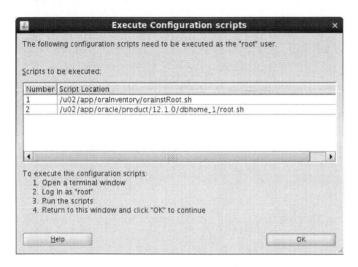

**Step 13: Finish** -- This is the screen you really want to see.

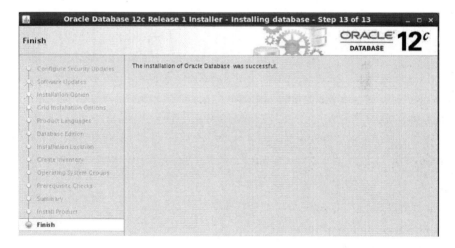

## Database Creation Assistant (DBCA)

In the bad old days, creating a database meant building a CREATE DATABASE statement that did everything you wanted it to. No one misses those days. Oracle's Database Configuration Assistant (DBCA) is a much simpler means of creating a database. In addition, once DBCA has completed, the database is immediately ready to use. By contrast, a database generated with the CREATE DATABASE statement still requires several scripts to be run before the database can be used. DBCA can be launched directly from the Oracle Installer, or it can be launched as a standalone tool at any point after the Oracle software has been installed.

DBCA has two modes of operation: interactive mode or noninteractive/silent mode. The interactive mode makes use of a graphical user interface and guides you through creating and configuring a database. The noninteractive mode allows you to create the database via a script. DBCA is run in noninteractive mode by specifying command-line arguments, a response file, or both. This chapter will cover only the interactive mode.

To start DBCA, log on to your computer as a member of the group that is authorized to install Oracle and to create and run the database. To start DBCA on UNIX or Linux, or at the command-line prompt in Microsoft Windows, enter the following command: dbca. The dbca executable is located in the ORACLE_HOME/bin directory. Once started, the DBCA user interface guides you through a step-by-step process to create a database.

**Step 1: Database Operation** -- This screen allows you to create a database, configure or delete a database (both grayed out in the screenshot below because no databases exist yet), manager templates for database creation, or manage pluggable databases (again grayed out because no CDB exists).

**Step 2: Creation Mode** -- In this step, you must choose the database name, storage type, location of the data files and fast recovery area, character set and the admin password. When using Oracle Enterprise Edition, you can also opt to create this as a container database. If you click the Advanced Mode radio button, you can customize many of the database parameters.

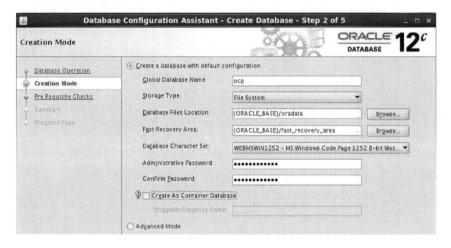

**Step 3: Pre Requisite Checks** -- DBCA verifies that all prerequisites have been met to create the database.

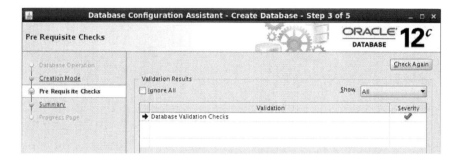

**Step 4: Summary** -- This screen shows details about how the database is going to be configured if you choose to complete the process at this point.

**Step 5: Progress Page** -- This screen allows you to follow the progress of DBCA as it builds the database.

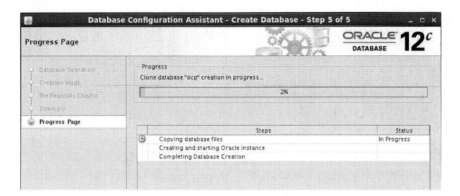

Once DBCA completes, the new database is started and ready to be used. You can connect to the database and begin creating users and objects immediately.

Ideally, you should run the utlrp.sql script after creating or upgrading a database. The script will recompile all PL/SQL modules that might be in an invalid state, including packages, procedures, and types. By default it will recompile the objects in parallel based on the CPU_COUNT of the system it is run on. This step is optional, but Oracle recommends that you do it during installation and not at a later date.

# Basics of Multitenant Container Database (CDB)

## Identify the benefits of the multitenant container database

Oracle 12c introduced a radical new architecture with the Multitenant option. The new architecture allows for Oracle to be provisioned as a 'Container' database (CDB) that can host multiple 'Pluggable' databases (PDBs) -- each of which can be added and removed from the CDB. Existing legacy Oracle databases can be adapted to become pluggable databases. The new PDBs in turn can continue to be accessed by other tiers without having to make changes to legacy applications.

There are a number of advantages to the Multitenant architecture, including:

- **Database Consolidation** -- Multiple pluggable databases can be stored in a single container database. When in a CDB, they share a single set of background processes, server and system memory while still maintaining complete separation of the data in each PDB. There is no added maintenance overhead or mingling of data as is the case with Virtual Private Databases. This makes it possible to store many more PDBs on a given hardware platform than individual Oracle databases using the legacy architecture.
- **Reduced Costs** -- Consolidating multiple databases can dramatically reduce the costs associated with hardware. In addition, a container database with a dozen PDBs requires considerably less maintenance than twelve individual databases. The result requires fewer personnel to maintain.
- **Rapid Implementation** -- Pluggable databases make it very easy to migrate or implement data and code. It requires very little time to plug a PDB into a CDB, unplug it, and then plug the PDB into a different CDB.
- **Simplified Management** -- With multiple PDBs in a single container database, it is simpler for database administrators to monitor and manage the physical database. There is only a single set of database files and one instance to maintain. This simplifies both backup strategies and disaster recovery scenarios.

- **Separation of administrative duties** -- Multitenant user accounts are either common, which allows them to connect to any container on which they have privileges, or local, and can only connect to a single PDB. DBA duties in turn can be split between CDB-level and PDB level. CDB administrators use a common account to manage the CDB. PDB administrators use local accounts to manage individual PDBs. Privileges exist only in the container for which they are granted. A local user on one PDB does not have privileges on other PDBs within the same CDB.
- **Simplified Tuning** -- Monitoring and tuning one database is much easier than monitoring and tuning a dozen databases.
- **Simplified Patching** -- Patching/upgrading a single database is much easier than doing so for a dozen databases.

## Explain root and multitenant architecture

The multitenant architecture is what allows an Oracle database to act as a container database that includes zero, one, or many PDBs. A container is a collection of schemas, objects, and related structures stored in a multitenant container database. A container is either a PDB or the root container (also called the root). Each PDB appears logically to an application as a separate database. Within a CDB, each PDB container must have a unique ID and name. PDBs isolate data and operations so that from the perspective of a user or application accessing it through Oracle Net, each PDB appears as if it were a traditional database.

Every container database has the following containers:

- **One root** -- The root container stores Oracle-supplied metadata (such as the source code for Oracle-supplied PL/SQL packages) and common users. A common user is a database user known in every container. The root container is named CDB$ROOT. All PDBs belong to the root. User data should never be stored in the root and the system-supplied schemas should never be altered. It is possible, however, to create common users and roles for database administration.

- **One seed PDB** -- The seed PDB is a system-supplied template that can be used to create new PDBs. The seed PDB is named PDB$SEED. You cannot add or modify objects in PDB$SEED.
- **Zero or more user-created PDBs** -- User-created PDBs are the entities that contain the data and code required for a specific set of features. No PDBs exist at the time the CDB is initially created. PDBs are added to the container database as needed. PDBs must be uniquely named within a CDB, and follow the same naming rules as service names. Moreover, because a PDB has a service with its own name, a PDB name must be unique across all CDBs whose services are exposed through a specific listener.

# Configuring and Creating CDBs and PDBs

## Create and configure a CDB

The steps involved in creating a container database are very much like those required to create a standard Oracle database. Prior to creating the CDB, you must take into account what the database will be used for and plan accordingly. Some of the recommended pre-creation actions include:

- Plan the tables and indexes for the pluggable databases (PDBs) that will be contained in the CDB and estimate the amount of space they will require.
- Plan the layout of the underlying operating system files for the CDB.
- Plan for the number of background processes that the CDB will require.
- Determine the global database name for the CDB to be set by the DB_NAME and DB_DOMAIN initialization parameters.
- Develop a backup and recovery strategy to protect the CDB from failure.
- Select an appropriate character set.
- Determine the appropriate initial size for the SYSAUX tablespace.

Before a new CDB can be created, the following prerequisites must be met:

- Oracle 12c must be installed with the database compatibility level to at least 12.0.0.
- Sufficient memory must be available to start the Oracle Database instance.
- Sufficient disk storage space must be available for the planned PDBs on the computer that runs Oracle Database.

The container database creation prepares several operating system files to work together as a CDB. A CDB can be created either during or after Oracle Database software installation. A CDB can be created either with the Database Configuration Assistant (DBCA) or with the CREATE DATABASE SQL statement. Oracle strongly recommends using the Database Configuration Assistant (DBCA) method. DBCA is a much easier method for doing so and the CDB is ready to use as soon as DBCA completes.

The Database Configuration Assistant can be launched by the Oracle Universal Installer or launched as a standalone tool at any time after Oracle Database installation. It is possible to create a CDB in interactive mode or noninteractive/silent mode. The interactive mode provides a graphical interface and guided workflow for the CDB creation process. Noninteractive mode enables you to script the creation of the CDB. Once the CDB has been created, DBCA can be used to plug new PDBs into it or unplug existing ones.

If you decide to use the CREATE DATABASE statement to create a CDB, there are additional actions that must be completed before the CDB will be operational. Namely, the standard PL/SQL packages must be installed and required views created against the data dictionary tables. The catcdb.sql script must be executed to perform these actions.

Using the CREATE DATABASE SQL statement to create a new CDB is very much like creating a non-CDB. It is a more labor-intensive process compared to creating a CDB than using DBCA. However, it allows CDBs to be created from within scripts, which is not possible when using DBCA. When using the CREATE DATABASE SQL statement, the names and locations of the root's files and the seed's files must be specified. The CREATE DATABASE statement uses the root's files (such as data files) to generate the names of the seed's files. After the CDB has been created, the seed and its files can be used to create new PDBs. The seed cannot be modified after it is created. The names and locations of the seed's files must be specified in one of the following ways:

- **SEED FILE_NAME_CONVERT** -- This clause specifies how to generate the names of the seed's files using the names of root's files. It can be used to specify one or more file name patterns and replacement file name patterns, in the following form: ('string1' , 'string2' , 'string3' , 'string4' , ...). In this form, the string2 file name pattern replaces the string1 file name pattern, and the string4 file name pattern replaces the string3 file name pattern. It is possible to specify as many pairs of file name pattern and replacement file name pattern strings as required. An odd number of strings will generate an error. The clause can also be set to NON, which means no file names should be converted (the same behavior as omitting the clause. The SEED FILE_NAME_CONVERT clause generates file names for the seed's files in the /oracle/pdbseed directory using file names in the /oracle/dbs directory. File name patterns specified in this initialization parameter cannot match files or directories managed by Oracle Managed Files.
- **Oracle Managed Files** -- When Oracle Managed Files is enabled, it can determine the names and locations of the seed's files.
- **PDB_FILE_NAME_CONVERT** -- The PDB_FILE_NAME_CONVERT initialization parameter can be used to specify the names and locations of the seed's files. If the PDB_FILE_NAME_CONVERT initialization parameter is included in the initialization parameter file when you create the CDB and neither of the other two methods is in place, it will determine the names of the seed's files.

When more than one of these methods is utilized, the method used is determined in the order of precedence shown above. If all three methods were specified in the CREATE DATABASE statement, only the specifications in the SEED FILE_NAME_CONVERT clause would be used.

## Create and configure a PDB

Prior to creating a PDB, several prerequisites must be met:

- The CDB must exist.
- The CDB must be in read/write mode.
- The current user must be a common user whose current container is the root.
- The current user must have the CREATE PLUGGABLE DATABASE system privilege.
- A PDB name must be selected that is unique to the CDB it will be plugged into and all the CDBs whose instances are reached through a specific listener.
- PDBs created in an Oracle Data Guard configuration with a physical standby database, have additional requirements. Reference the Oracle Data Guard Concepts and Administration manual for more information.

There are four different methods for creating a pluggable database (PDB) in a multitenant container database (CDB):

- **Using the seed** -- The files associated with the seed are copied to a new location and associated with the new PDB.
- **Cloning an existing PDB** -- An existing PDB can be cloned and plugged into the CDB. The PDB to be used as the source can either be in the local CDB or in a remote CDB. All of the files associated with the source PDB are copied to a new location and associated with the new PDB.
- **Plugging in an unplugged PDB** -- The XML metadata file that describes an unplugged PDB plus its associated files are plugged into the CDB.
- **Converting a non-CDB** -- The DBMS_PDB package can create an unplugged PDB from an Oracle Database 12c non-CDB. The newly-created PDB can then be plugged into a CDB.

All four techniques make use of the CREATE PLUGGABLE DATABASE statement at some point. This statement is used for both copying a database and for plugging a PDB in to a CDB as required. The statement has optional clauses that can be used to set several aspects of the PDB:

- **Storage** – The STORAGE clause specifies the amount of storage that can be used by all tablespaces that belong to the PDB and the amount of storage in the default temporary tablespace shared by all PDBs that can be used by sessions connected to the PDB. If STORAGE UNLIMITED is set, or if there is no STORAGE clause, the PDB has no storage limits.
- **File Locations** -- There are three clauses that affect the file names used for a PDB. The PATH_PREFIX clause can be used to ensure that a PDB's files reside in a specific directory and its subdirectories when relative paths are used for directory objects and certain initialization parameters. The FILE_NAME_CONVERT clause specifies the names of the PDB's files after the PDB is plugged into the CDB. The SOURCE_FILE_NAME_CONVERT clause specifies the names of a PDB's files before the PDB is plugged into the CDB.
- **Temp File Reuse** -- The TEMPFILE REUSE clause specifies that an existing temp file in the target location is reused if one exists. If this clause is specified, and there is no temp file in the target location, Oracle will create a new temp file. If the clause is not specified, Oracle will attempt to create a new temp file for the PDB. If a file exists with the same name as the new temp file in the target location, an error will be generated, and the PDB creation will fail.

**Creating a PDB Using the Seed**

The CREATE PLUGGABLE DATABASE statement can be used to create a PDB in a CDB using the files of the seed. When creating a new PDB from the seed, a PDB administrator must be specified in the CREATE PLUGGABLE DATABASE statement. The new database will be created with three tablespaces: SYSTEM, SYSAUX, and TEMP. The administrator is created as a local user in the PDB and granted the PDB_DBA role. To create a PDB from the seed:

- In SQL*Plus, ensure that the current container is the root.
- Run the CREATE PLUGGABLE DATABASE statement, and specify a local administrator for the PDB. Specify other clauses when they are required.
- Open the new PDB in read/write mode that that Oracle can complete the integration of the new PDB into the CDB.
- Back up the PDB.

An example of this method (with none of the optional clauses) is:

```
CREATE PLUGGABLE DATABASE ocp_pdb ADMIN USER ocp_adm IDENTIFIED BY
password;
```

### Cloning a PDB

The CREATE PLUGGABLE DATABASE statement can be used to clone a PDB. When cloning an existing PDB, the FROM clause will specify the source PDB to be cloned. The source PDB can be in the local CDB or in a remote CDB. In order to clone a PDB, the current user must have the CREATE PLUGGABLE DATABASE system privilege in both the root and the source PDB and the source PDB must be open in read-only mode. To clone a PDB:

- In SQL*Plus, ensure that the current container is the root.
- Run the CREATE PLUGGABLE DATABASE statement, and specify the source PDB in the FROM clause. Specify other clauses when they are required.
- Open the new PDB in read/write mode.
- Back up the PDB.

An example of the syntax for cloning a PDB is:

```
CREATE PLUGGABLE DATABASE pdb2 FROM pdb1
PATH_PREFIX = '/u02/oracle/pdb2'
FILE_NAME_CONVERT = ('/u01/oracle/pdb1/', '/u02/oracle/pdb2/');
```

## Plugging an Unplugged PDB into a CDB

This technique uses the XML metadata file of an existing PDB along with its associated files to plug it into the CDB. The USING clause of the CREATE PLUGGABLE DATABASE statement specifies the XML metadata file. The XML file in turn contains the locations of the PDB's files. To plug in an unplugged PDB:

- In SQL*Plus, ensure that the current container is the root.
- (Optional) Run the DBMS_PDB.CHECK_PLUG_COMPATIBILITY function to determine whether the unplugged PDB is compatible with the CDB.
- Run the CREATE PLUGGABLE DATABASE statement, and specify the XML file in the USING clause. Specify other clauses when they are required.
- Open the new PDB in read/write mode.
- Back up the PDB.

An example of the syntax for plugging in an unplugged PDB is:

```
CREATE PLUGGABLE DATABASE ocp_pdb USING '/u01/usr/ocp_pdb.xml'
NOCOPY TEMPFILE REUSE;
```

## Creating a PDB Using a Non-CDB

It is possible to move a non-CDB into a PDB via three different methods:

- **DBMS_PDB** -- The DBMS_PDB package can be used to generate an XML metadata file. This file describes the database files of the non-CDB . It can then be plugged into a CDB using the XML file as described above. In order to use this technique, the non-CDB must be from an Oracle 12c Database. Older databases must be upgraded to Oracle Database 12c in order to use this technique.
- **Oracle Data Pump** -- With this method, Oracle Data Pump is used to export the data from the non-CDB database so that it can then be imported into a PDB.

- **Goldengate replication** -- In this method data is replicated from the non-CDB to a PDB. When the PDB catches up with the non-CDB, you fail over to the PDB.

## Drop a PDB

The DROP PLUGGABLE DATABASE statement is used to drop a PDB. A PDB might be dropped in order to move it to another CDB or when it is no longer needed. When a PDB is dropped, the control file of the CDB is modified to eliminate all references to it. Any archived redo log files and backups that are associated with the PDB are not removed by the DROP statement. Oracle Recovery Manager (RMAN) can be used to remove them. When a PDB is dropped, it is possible to either keep or delete the data files associated with it by using one of the following clauses:

- **KEEP DATAFILES** -- This is the default, and retains the data files. The PDB's temp file is removed even when KEEP DATAFILES is specified because it is no longer needed.
- **INCLUDING DATAFILES** -- This option removes the data files from disk. For a PDB that was created with the SNAPSHOT COPY clause, INCLUDING DATAFILES must be specified when dropping the PDB.

In order to drop a PDB, the following prerequisites must be met:

- The PDB must be in mounted mode or it must be unplugged.
- The current user must have SYSDBA or SYSOPER administrative privilege commonly granted or locally granted in the PDB. The session must have been connected using the AS SYSDBA or AS SYSOPER clause.

To drop a PDB:

1. In SQL*Plus, ensure that the current container is the root.
2. Run the DROP PLUGGABLE DATABASE statement and specify the PDB to drop.

```
DROP PLUGGABLE DATABASE ocpdb
INCLUDING DATAFILES;
```

# Migrate a non-CDB to a PDB database

As mentioned in the previous section, three methods exist for moving a non-CDB into a PDB: the DBMS_PDB package, Oracle Data Pump, and Goldengate replication. This section will deal with using the DBMS_PDB.DESCRIBE procedure of the DBMS_PDB package. Oracle Data Pump is discussed in a later section and GoldenGate is outside the scope of this exam.

To move a non-CDB into a PDB using the DBMS_PDB package, the CDB must be in a transactionally-consistent state. In addition, it must be placed in read-only mode. Once the non-CDB is read-only, connect to the database, and execute the DBMS_PDB.DESCRIBE procedure. This procedure will construct an XML file that describes the non-CDB. The following example will generate an XML file named ocp_db.xml in the /u01/oracle directory:

```
BEGIN
DBMS_PDB.DESCRIBE(
  pdb_descr_file => '/u01/oracle/ocp_db.xml');
END;
/
```

Once the procedure has completed and the XML file has been created, the XML file and the non-CDB's database files can be plugged into a CDB. Shut down the non-CDB and then issue the CREATE PLUGGABLE DATABASE statement with the appropriate clauses, for example:

```
CREATE PLUGGABLE DATABASE ncdb USING '/u01/oracle/ocp_db.xml'
COPY
FILE_NAME_CONVERT = ('/u01/oracle/dbs/', '/u02/oracle/ocp_db/');
```

Before opening the new PDB for the first time, you must run the ORACLE_HOME/rdbms/admin/noncdb_to_pdb.sql script. This script is only required when converting non-CDB databases into a PDB.

```
@$ORACLE_HOME/rdbms/admin/noncdb_to_pdb.sql
```

After running the script, the new PDB must be opened in read/write mode for Oracle Database to complete the integration of the new PDB into the CDB. An error is returned if you attempt o open the PDB in read-only mode. Once the database has been opened in read-write mode, you should immediately take a backup of the new PDB.

# Managing CDBs and PDBs

## Establish connection to a CDB/PDB

Client applications connecting to a CDB can access the root or a PDB through database services. Database services have an optional PDB property. At the time each new PDB is created, a new default service with the same name as the PDB will be created automatically. When Oracle Net Services is configured properly, it is possible to use the service name to access the PDB using the easy connect syntax or the net service name from the tnsnames.ora file. When a connection is submitted using a service with a non-null PDB property, the user name for the session is resolved in the context of the specified PDB. If no service is specified or a service name with a NULL PDB property is used, the user name will be resolved in the context of the root.

If two or more CDBs on the same computer system use the same listener and they contain two or more PDBs with the same service name, using that service name will connect randomly to one of the PDBs using it. All service names for PDBs should be unique on a given system, or each CDB should use a separate listener.

It is possible to connect to a container by using the SQL*Plus CONNECT command. Alternately, it is possible to switch into a container with an ALTER SESSION SET CONTAINER SQL statement. The CONNECT command can be used to connect either to the root or to a PDB in a CDB. Any of the following techniques are valid for connecting to the root using the SQL*Plus CONNECT command:

- Local connection
- Local connection with operating system authentication
- Database connection using easy connect
- Database connection using a net service name
- Remote database connection using external authentication

In order for a user to connect to the root, they must be a common user and that user must have been granted CREATE SESSION privilege in the root. To connect to the root using the SQL*Plus CONNECT command, you must start SQL*Plus with the /NOLOG argument:

```
sqlplus /nolog
```

Once in SQL*Plus, you can connect to the root by various methods:

- **Connecting with a Local Connection**
  ```
  connect username/password
  ```

- **Connecting with Operating System Authentication**
  ```
  connect / as sysdba
  ```

- **Connecting with a Net Service Name**
  ```
  connect username/password@ocp_db
  ```

Either of the following techniques can be used to connect to a PDB with the SQL*Plus CONNECT command:

- Database connection using easy connect
- Database connection using a net service name

In order to connect to a PDB, a user must be a common user of the CDB with CREATE SESSION granted either commonly or locally in the PDB, or a local user in the PDB with CREATE SESSION granted. Only a user with SYSDBA, SYSOPER, SYSBACKUP, or SYSDG privilege can connect to a PDB that is in mounted mode. To connect to a PDB using the SQL*Plus CONNECT command, you must start SQL*Plus with the /NOLOG argument:

```
sqlplus /nolog
```

The following command connects to the candidate local user in the ocp_db PDB:

```
CONNECT candidate@ocp_db
```

When a session is connected to a container as a common user, the following statement can be used to switch to a different container:

```
ALTER SESSION SET CONTAINER = container_name
```

The container_name, can be any one of the following:

- CDB$ROOT to switch to the root
- PDB$SEED to switch to the seed
- A PDB name to switch to the PDB

## Start up and shut down a CDB/PDB

Unless being operated in a Real Application Clusters environment, a CDB runs with a single instance. The startup process for a CDB instance is same as that for non-CDB databases. STARTUP NOMOUNT, STARTUP MOUNT, and STARTUP OPEN all function in a CDB and have the effect on the Container Database that they would on a non-CDB. However, the status of the PDBs within the CDB is not always the same. You need to be connected to the root of the CDB with SYSDBA privileges in order to start the instance. Once the instance has been started, you may use the V$PDBS view to determine the status of PDBs.

- **NOMOUNT** -- When the CDB is in NOMOUNT status, the instance is started, but the PDBs have no status. Querying the V$PDBS view will return no rows.

- **MOUNT** -- When the CDB is in MOUNT status, the control files for the instance will be opened. The Root and all of the PDBs will be in a status of MOUNTED.
- **OPEN** -- When the CDB is initially set to OPN, the root will be opened. The SEEB PDB will be opened in read-only mode. All other PDBs in the CDB will still be in MOUNTED status.

Once the CDB is opened, it is possible to open the PDBs individually or all at once:

```
ALTER PLUGGABLE DATABASE ocp_db OPEN;
ALTER PLUGGABLE DATABASE ALL OPEN;
```

A CDB instance is shut down in the same fashion that a non-CDB instance is. To shut the instance down, the following requirements must be met:

- It must be mounted or open
- The current user must be a common user with SYSDBA, SYSOPER, SYSBACKUP, or SYSDG administrative privilege
- The current container must be the root.

The open mode of a PDB can be altered using the ALTER PLUGGABLE DATABASE SQL statement or the SQL*Plus STARTUP command. The possible modes for PDBs are:

- **OPEN READ WRITE** -- This mode allows queries and user transactions to proceed and allows users to generate redo logs.
- **OPEN READ ONLY** -- This mode allows queries but does not allow user changes.
- **OPEN MIGRATE** -- This mode allows you to run database upgrade scripts on the PDB. A PDB is in this mode after an ALTER DATABASE OPEN UPGRADE is run.
- **MOUNTED** -- A PDB is in mounted mode behaves like a non-CDB in mounted mode. No changes are allowed to objects and it is accessible only to database administrators.

When the current container is the root, an ALTER PLUGGABLE DATABASE statement with a pdb_change_state clause modifies the open mode of the specified PDBs. When a PDB is opened using the ALTER PLUGGABLE DATABASE OPEN statement, READ WRITE is the default unless the PDB belongs to a CDB that is used as a physical standby database, in which case READ ONLY is the default. The PDBs to be modified by the ALTER statement can be specified in the following ways:

- List one or more PDBs separated by commas.
- Specify ALL to modify all of the PDBs.
- Specify ALL EXCEPT to modify all of the PDBs, except for the PDBs listed.

Some examples of this statement are:

```
ALTER PLUGGABLE DATABASE ocp_db, test_db OPEN READ WRITE;

ALTER PLUGGABLE DATABASE ocp_db OPEN READ ONLY RESTRICTED;

ALTER PLUGGABLE DATABASE ALL OPEN READ WRITE;
```

When the current container is the root it is also possible to use the STARTUP PLUGGABLE DATABASE command to open a single PDB. The STARTUP PLUGGABLE DATABASE statement has the following options:

- **FORCE** -- Closes an open PDB before re-opening it in read/write mode.
- **RESTRICT** -- Enables only users with the RESTRICTED SESSION system privilege in the PDB to access the PDB.
- **OPEN** -- Opens the PDB in either read/write mode or read-only mode. You can specify OPEN READ WRITE or OPEN READ ONLY. When no option is specified, READ WRITE is the default.

## Some examples of this statement are:

```
STARTUP PLUGGABLE DATABASE ocp_db OPEN

STARTUP PLUGGABLE DATABASE ocp_db RESTRICT

STARTUP PLUGGABLE DATABASE ocp_db OPEN READ ONLY

STARTUP PLUGGABLE DATABASE ocp_db FORCE
```

The ALTER PLUGGABLE DATABASE can also be used to close one or more PDBs. To close a PDB, connect to the root as SYSOPER or SYSDBA and issue an ALTER PLUGGABLE DATABASE CLOSE statement, specifying the PDB or PDBs to be closed. If the command is issued with the IMMEDIATE keyword, transactions in the selected PDBs are rolled back and the sessions disconnected. If the IMMEDIATE keyword is omitted, the statement hangs until all sessions have disconnected from the PDB. All of the data files of the PDB will be closed and it will be inaccessible to users. When connected to PDB, issuing a SHUTDOWN IMMEDIATE is equivalent to ALTER PLUGGABLE DATABASE CLOSE.

## Some examples of this statement are:

```
ALTER PLUGGABLE DATABASE ocp_db, test_db CLOSE;

ALTER PLUGGABLE DATABASE ALL CLOSE;

ALTER PLUGGABLE DATABASE ALL EXCEPT testdb CLOSE IMMEDIATE;
```

## Change instance parameters for a CDB/PDB

A CDB will contain only a single SPFILE no matter how many PDBs it contains. Any initialization parameters specified at the root level apply to the root and will be the default value for any PDBs it contains. Many (but not all) initialization parameters can also be set at the PDB level. The parameters that are modifiable for PDBs can be located with the following query:

```
SELECT name
FROM    v$system_parameter
WHERE   ispdb_modifiable = 'TRUE'
ORDER BY name;
```

Any of the initialization parameters listed by this query that are not set independently for a PDB will be inherited from the parameter value set at the root. Values from the list can be set at the PDB level with the ALTER SYSTEM command. When the SCOPE is set to SPFILE or BOTH, the values will be retained across PDB close/open and across bouncing the CDB instance. Parameters set at this level will also travel with clone and unplug/plug operations. Any initialization parameters that do not show up in the above query can be set for the root only.

# Managing Tablespaces, Common and Local Users, Privileges and Roles

## Manage tablespaces in a CDB/PDB

Tablespaces in a multitenant environment serve the same purpose and for the most part are treated in the same fashion as tablespaces in a non-CDB. The syntax for creating and altering tablespaces is largely unchanged. There are a few considerations for tablespaces in a CDB:

- A permanent tablespace can be associated with only one container.
- When you create a tablespace in a container, the tablespace is associated with that container.
- A CDB can have only one active undo tablespace or one active undo tablespace for each instance of an Oracle RAC CDB.
- There is one default temporary tablespace for an entire CDB. The root and the PDBs can use this temporary tablespace. Optionally, each PDB can also have its own default temporary tablespace.

Because a permanent tablespace can be associated with only a single container, each container must have its own default permanent tablespace. They cannot be shared between containers. Users connected to a given container who are not explicitly assigned a tablespace will use that container's default permanent tablespace. When connected to the CDB, the command to set the default permanent tablespace would be:

```
ALTER DATABASE DEFAULT TABLESPACE tbs_users_cdb;
```

While connected to a PDB, the 'ALTER DATABASE' command is still retained for backward compatibility, but the preferred command would be:

```
ALTER PLUGGABLE DATABASE DEFAULT TABLESPACE tbs_users_pdb;
```

A CDB will have only a single default temporary tablespace (or tablespace group). In order to create or modify this temporary tablespace, the current container must be the root. It is possible to have additional temporary tablespaces in the root, and to assign specific users to them. Likewise, each PDB can contain one default temporary tablespace and additional temporary tablespaces that can be assigned specific users. When a PDB is unplugged from a CDB, its temporary tablespaces are also unplugged.

## Manage users and privileges for CDB/PDB

A common user is a database user that has the same identity in the root and in every existing and future PDB. Common users can connect to and perform operations within the root, and within any PDB in which it has been granted privileges. A user connected to the root can perform certain operations, such as ALTER PLUGGABLE DATABASE, CREATE USER, CREATE ROLE, that affect other pluggable databases (PDBs). However, most privileges can only be exercised within the current container. Users must first switch to the PDB where the action is to be taken, and then exercise their privileges from there. For example, a common user cannot query tables or views in a PDB when it is not the current container.

**Creating a common user account:**

- You must be connected to the root and have the commonly granted CREATE USER system privilege.
- The session's current container must be CDB$ROOT.
- The name of the common user must start with C## or c## and contain only ASCII or EDCDIC characters.
- To explicitly designate a user account as a common user, in the CREATE USER statement, specify CONTAINER=ALL. When logged into the root, if the CONTAINER clause is omitted, CONTAINER=ALL is implied.

No objects should be created in the schemas of common users. They cannot be shared across PDB boundaries and can cause problems during plug-in and unplug operations. The following example creates a common user account and grants the user the SET CONTAINER and CREATE SESSION privileges (common users must have these privileges to navigate between containers):

```
CREATE USER c##ocp_admin
  IDENTIFIED BY password
  DEFAULT TABLESPACE ts_cdb_users
  QUOTA 100M ON ts_cdb_users
  TEMPORARY TABLESPACE temp_ts
  CONTAINER = ALL;
GRANT SET CONTAINER, CREATE SESSION
  TO c##ocp_admin CONTAINER = ALL;
```

**Creating a local user account:**

Local user accounts exist only in the PDB that they are created in. They cannot connect to or be granted privileges in other PDBs. It is possible, of course, to create a user of the same name in multiple PDBs, but the accounts share nothing except the name. To create a local user account:

- You must be connected to the PDB in which you want to create the account, and have the CREATE USER privilege.
- The name of the local user must not start with C## or c##.
- The clause CONTAINER=CURRENT can be included in the CREATE USER statement to explicitly specify the user as a local user. When connected to a PDB, if the clause is omitted, CONTAINER=CURRENT is implied.

```
CREATE USER ocp_user
  IDENTIFIED BY password
  DEFAULT TABLESPACE ts_pdb_users
  QUOTA 100M ON ts_pdb_users
  TEMPORARY TABLESPACE temp_ts
  PROFILE ocp_profile
  CONTAINER = CURRENT;
```

Common users and local users can grant privileges to one another. A given privilege (i.e. CREATE ANY TABLE) is neither common nor local by itself. If CREATE ANY TABLE is granted commonly, then it becomes a common privilege, and if granted locally, it becomes a local privilege.

**Commonly granted privileges:**

- A privilege that is granted commonly can be used in every existing and future container.
- Only common users can grant privileges commonly, and only to a common user or common role.
- The grantor must be connected to the root and must specify CONTAINER=ALL in the GRANT statement.
- Can include system and object privileges.
- Should never be granted to PUBLIC.

**Locally granted privileges:**

- A privilege granted locally can be used only in the container in which it was granted, even when granted in the root.
- Both common users and local users can grant privileges locally.
- A common user and a local user can grant privileges to other common or local roles.
- The grantor must be connected to the container and must specify CONTAINER=CURRENT in the GRANT statement.
- Any user can grant a privilege locally to any other user or role (both common and local) or to the PUBLIC role.

The CONTAINER clause in a GRANT or REVOKE statement determines where a privilege is granted to or revoked from. When the CONTAINER is set to ALL, the statement applies the privilege to all existing and future containers. Using CURRENT in the clause will apply the privilege to the local container. The value will default to CURRENT if the clause is omitted except when connected to the root, when the default will be ALL. The following example grants the CREATE TABLE privilege to common user c##ocp_admin. After the grant, the user will be able to use the privilege in all existing and future containers.

```
GRANT CREATE TABLE TO c##ocp_admin CONTAINER=ALL;
```

Common roles are created in the root and are known in all existing and future containers. All Oracle-supplied predefined roles are common roles. Local roles exist in only the PDB they were created in and can only be used there. Local roles cannot have any commonly granted privileges.

- Common users can both create and grant common roles to other common and local users.
- A common role can be granted to a common user either commonly or locally.
- If a common role is granted to a local user, the privileges from the role apply only to the local user's PDB.
- Local users cannot create common roles
- Local users can grant common roles to common and local users.

If the following requirements are met, commonly granted privileges that have been made to a common role apply in the root and all current and future PDBs to which the grantor can connect:

- Both the grantor and the grantee are common users.
- The grantor possesses the commonly granted SET CONTAINER privilege and the ADMIN OPTION for the common role.
- The GRANT statement contains the CONTAINER=ALL clause.

The name given to user-created common roles must start with C## or c## and contain only ASCII or EDCDIC characters (the C## rule does not apply to Oracle-supplied roles, such as DBA or RESOURCE). When the role is created, the CONTAINER clause must be set to ALL. Except when logged in to the root, omitting this clause from the CREATE ROLE statement creates a local role in the current PDB. If the CONTAINER clause is omitted when logged in to the root, by default the role is created as a common role. The following example creates the c##ocp_admin common role:

```
CREATE ROLE c##ocp_admin CONTAINER=ALL;
```

# Backup, Recovery and Flashback for a CDB/PDB

## Perform backup of CDB and PDB

There is a full range of capabilities for backing up Oracle databases in a multitenant environment through RMAN and Enterprise Manager Cloud Control. If is possible to back up and recover a complete CDB, just the root of the CDB, or to back up any or all of the PDBs. It is also possible to back up and recover individual tablespaces and data files in a single PDB. Backing up each element of a container database individually (the root and each PDB) is functionally equivalent in terms of recoverability to backing up the entire CDB.

The steps for backing up an entire CDB are equivalent to performing a full database backup of a non-CDB. When the entire CDB is backed up, RMAN backs up the root, all the PDBs, and the archived redo logs. From the resulting backup, it is possible to recover the whole CDB, the root only, or combination of PDBs contained in the CDB backup. To back up a CDB, you must start RMAN and connect to the root of the CDB as a common user with the SYSBACKUP or SYSDBA privilege and to a recovery catalog (if used). The database must be either mounted or open. You can then issue the appropriate backup options from the RMAN prompt:

Back up the entire CDB:

```
RMAN> BACKUP DATABASE;
```

Back up the database, switch the online redo logs, and include archived logs in the backup:

```
RMAN> BACKUP DATABASE PLUS ARCHIVELOG;
```

## Back Up the Root

```
RMAN> BACKUP DATABASE ROOT;
```

## Back Up a PDB

There are two approaches to backing up a PDB with RMAN:

- Connect to the root and then issue the BACKUP PLUGGABLE DATABASE command from the RMAN prompt. This method can be used to back up one or more PDBs.

  ```
  RMAN> BACKUP PLUGGABLE DATABASE ocprep;

  RMAN> BACKUP PLUGGABLE DATABASE ocprep, testdb;
  ```

- Connect to the PDB and then issue the following command from the RMAN prompt:

  ```
  RMAN> BACKUP DATABASE;
  ```

# Perform recovery of CDB and PDB

When recovering a container database, it is possible to recover the entire CDB, only the root, only a single PDB, or just a portion of a PDB such as a tablespace or datafile. When the whole CDB is recovered, the root and all PDBs are recovered in a single operation.

To recover the entire CDB, you use the RMAN commands RESTORE and RECOVER. RMAN will automatically restore the backups of any required archived redo logs during the recovery operation. If the backup is stored on a media manager, then any required channels must be configured so that RMAN can access the backup files. To recover an entire CDB, you must start RMAN and connect to the root of the CDB as a common user with the SYSBACKUP or SYSDBA privilege and to a recovery catalog (if used). The following commands will restore and recover the entire CDB:

```
RESTORE DATABASE;
RECOVER DATABASE;
```

You can delete any archived redo logs that were restored from disk for the recovery operation (once they are no longer needed for recovery) by using the following command:

```
RECOVER DATABASE DELETE ARCHIVELOG;
```

It is possible to recover only the root if a user error or data corruption occurs that is specific to the root. However, Oracle strongly recommends that you recover all PDBs after recovering the root. This will eliminate the possibility of introducing metadata inconsistencies among the root and the PDBs. As a general rule, it is preferable to recover the whole CDB. To recover the root, you must be connected to the root from RMAN as a common user with the SYSDBA or SYSBACKUP privilege and the CDB must be in MOUNT mode.

- If required, use the CONFIGURE command to configure the default device type and automatic channels.
- Restore and recover the root with the following commands:

```
RESTORE DATABASE ROOT;
RECOVER DATABASE ROOT;
```

- Examine the output from RMAN to verify that media recovery was successful. Oracle strongly recommends at this point that you recover all of the PDBs, including the seed. To do this, issue the RESTORE PLUGGABLE DATABASE and RECOVER PLUGGABLE DATABASE commands.

```
RESTORE PLUGGABLE DATABASE 'PDB$SEED', ocprep, testdb;
RECOVER PLUGGABLE DATABASE 'PDB$SEED', ocprep, testdb;
```

- Examine the output from RMAN to verify that media recovery was successful. If it was successful, open the CDB and all PDBs.

```
ALTER DATABASE OPEN;
ALTER PLUGGABLE DATABASE ALL OPEN;
```

It is possible to perform a complete recovery on a given PDB, or multiple PDBs without affecting operations of other open PDBs in the same container database. It is possible to recover a PDB in RMAN while connected to the root or while connected to the PDB. While connected to the root, you would use the RESTORE PLUGGABLE DATABASE and RECOVER PLUGGABLE DATABASE commands (as shown in the example above). With these commands, you can recover multiple pluggable databases at once. When connected to the PDB you would use the RESTORE DATABASE and RECOVER DATABASE commands. Only one PDB can be recovered at a time using this method. The following steps will recover the ocprep PDB while connected to the root from RMAN as a common user with the SYSDBA or SYSBACKUP privilege:

- Close the PDBs to be recovered.

```
ALTER PLUGGABLE DATABASE ocprep CLOSE;
```

- If the PDB has missing data files an error will occur and the PDB cannot be closed. You must connect to the PDB with missing data file(s) and take them offline so that the PDB can be closed. The following command takes the data file 8 offline:

```
ALTER PLUGGABLE DATABASE DATAFILE 8 OFFLINE;
```

- If required, use the CONFIGURE command to configure the default device type and automatic channels.
- Restore and recover the PDB with the following commands:

```
RESTORE PLUGGABLE DATABASE ocprep;
RECOVER PLUGGABLE DATABASE ocprep;
```

- If any data files were taken offline in Step 2, bring these data files back online, for example:

```
ALTER PLUGGABLE DATABASE DATAFILE 8 ONLINE;
```

- Examine the output from RMAN to verify that media recovery was successful. If it was successful, open the PDB(s).

```
ALTER PLUGGABLE DATABASE ocprep OPEN;
```

To recover a single PDB while connected to it, you connect to the PDB from RMAN as a local user with SYSDBA system privilege.

- Close the PDB.

  ```
  ALTER PLUGGABLE DATABASE CLOSE;
  ```

- If the PDB has missing data files an error will occur and the PDB cannot be closed. You must connect to the PDB with missing data file(s) and take them offline so that the PDB can be closed. The following command takes the data file 8 offline:

  ```
  ALTER DATABASE DATAFILE 8 OFFLINE;
  ```

- If required, use the CONFIGURE command to configure the default device type and automatic channels.
- Restore and recover the PDB with the following commands:

  ```
  RESTORE DATABASE;
  RECOVER DATABASE;
  ```

- If any data files were taken offline in Step 2, connect to that PDB and bring these data files back online, for example:

  ```
  ALTER DATABASE DATAFILE 8 ONLINE;
  ```

- Examine the output from RMAN to verify that media recovery was successful. If it was successful, open the PDB(s).

  ```
  ALTER PLUGGABLE DATABASE OPEN;
  ```

# Perform Flashback for a CDB

It is possible to perform Flashback Database Operations on a CDB as you would on a non-CDB. One exception is performing a flashback when one or more of the PDBs were recovered using Point-In-Time-Recovery. In order to maintain backward compatibility, Flashback Database operations on a CDB may not be permitted if point-in-time recovery has been performed on any of its PDBs. When this has occurred, it is not possible to directly rewind the CDB to a point earlier than where the DBPITR was performed for the PDB. Attempting to flashback to an earlier point will generate the following error:

```
ORA-39866: Data files for pluggable database <PDB_name> must be
offline to flashback across a PDB point-in-time recovery
```

If it is necessary to flashback the CDB to a point earlier than the DBPITR of the PDB, you must perform the following steps:

- Start RMAN and connect to the root as a user with the SYSBACKUP or SYSDBA privilege.
- Determine the target time to which the CDB must be recovered.
- Take all files that correspond to the PDB for which PITR was performed offline.
- Rewind the CDB to the desired target time. The PDB whose files are offline will not be affected.
- Recover the PDB for which PITR was performed using the RESTORE PLUGGABLE DATABASE and RECOVER PLUGGABLE DATABASE commands.

# Information Lifecycle Management and Storage Enhancements

## Use ILM features

Information Lifecycle Management (ILM) is the act of managing data from creation/acquisition to archival or deletion. Oracle 12c offers two new ILM features that allow the database to intelligently manage space usage: Heat Map and Automatic Data Optimization.

### Heat Map

In any given database, not every piece of data is accessed in the same fashion or with the same frequency. Data which is accessed frequently must be on storage media that offers the best possible performance. By contrast, data which is seldom accessed could be kept on storage that has a lower performance without materially affecting the performance of the database. The fastest storage is inevitably the most expensive, so cost factors often make it impractical to be used to store everything in a given database.

Storage tiering is the act of deploying data on multiple types of storage media. When storage tiering is used, the ideal situation is to have the most frequently accessed data stored on the fastest media and the least-frequently accessed data on the slowest. The new Heat Map feature of Oracle is specifically designed for this purpose. It automatically tracks usage information at the row and segment levels. When data is modified, the times are tracked at the row level and aggregated to the block level. Modification times, full table scan times, and index lookup times are all tracked at the segment level. The end result is that using Heat Map, it is possible to obtain a detailed view of how data is being accessed, and how the access patterns change over time.

**Automatic Data Optimization**

The Automatic Data Optimization (ADO) feature enables database administrators to create policies for data compression and data movement. One of the features of ADO is Smart Compression, which makes use of information from the Heat Map to associate compression policies and compression levels with the way the data is utilized. Periodically the database will evaluate ADO policies and use Heat Map information to determine when to move and/or compress data. Once enabled, ADO works in the background during maintenance windows without user intervention, but can also be executed manually by the DBA. ADO policies can be specified at the segment or row level for tables and table partitions.

# Perform tracking and automated data placement

To implement your ILM strategy, you can use Heat Map in Oracle Database to track data access and modification. Enabling the Heat Map in Oracle is one way of implementing an ILM strategy. Heat Map tracking can be enabled and disabled at the system or session level with the ALTER SYSTEM or ALTER SESSION statements using the HEAT_MAP clause. Once enabled, all accesses to objects in all tablespaces except SYSTEM and SYSAUX are tracked by the in-memory activity tracking module. The following SQL statements enable and disable Heat Map tracking for the database instance respectively.

```
ALTER SYSTEM SET HEAT_MAP = ON;

ALTER SYSTEM SET HEAT_MAP = OFF;
```

There are several views that can be used to analyze the data returned by Oracle's Heat Map tracking:

- **V$HEAT_MAP_SEGMENT** -- Displays real-time segment access information.
- **DBA_HEAT_MAP_SEGMENT** -- Displays the latest segment access time for all segments.
- **DBA_HEAT_MAP_SEG_HISTOGRAM** -- Displays segment access information for all segments.
- **DBA_HEATMAP_TOP_OBJECTS** -- Displays heat map information for the top 1000 objects.
- **DBA_HEATMAP_TOP_TABLESPACES** -- Displays heat map information for the top 100 tablespaces.

In order to automatically move data between different storage tiers, you must specify one or more Automatic Data Optimization (ADO) policies. ADO policies can be specified at the row, segment, and tablespace level either at the time of creation or via an ALTER statement for existing objects. ADO policies can be specified with a scope of SEGMENT, ROW, or GROUP. The following statement shows ILM policies for the current user:

```
SELECT policy_name, policy_type, enabled
FROM   user_impolicies;
```

The SQL CREATE and ALTER TABLE statements have an optional ILM clause that allows an ADO policy to be created, deleted, enabled or disabled. The policy clause will determine policy used to compress or alter the storage tiering for that object. ILM ADO policies are given a system-generated name, such P1, P2, ... Pn.

Segment level policies execute only a single time. Once the policy has executed successfully, it will be disabled and is never evaluated again unless it is explicitly re-enabled. Row level policies are not disabled after a successful execution and will execute multiple times.

The default mappings for compression that can be applied to group policies are:

- **COMPRESS ADVANCED** on a heap table maps to standard compression for indexes and LOW for LOB segments.
- **COMPRESS FOR QUERY LOW/QUERY HIGH** on a heap table maps to standard compression for indexes and MEDIUM for LOB segments.
- **COMPRESS FOR ARCHIVE LOW/ARCHIVE HIGH** on a heap table maps to standard compression for indexes and HIGH for LOB segments.

The following examples add ILM policies to a partition of the HR.SALES table:

```
ALTER TABLE hr.sales MODIFY PARTITION sales_q1_2002
  ILM ADD POLICY ROW STORE COMPRESS ADVANCED ROW
  AFTER 45 DAYS OF NO MODIFICATION;

ALTER TABLE hr.sales MODIFY PARTITION sales_q1_2001
  ILM ADD POLICY COMPRESS FOR ARCHIVE HIGH SEGMENT
  AFTER 9 MONTHS OF NO MODIFICATION;

ALTER TABLE hr.sales MODIFY PARTITION sales_q1_2000
    ILM ADD POLICY COMPRESS FOR ARCHIVE HIGH SEGMENT
    AFTER 12 MONTHS OF NO ACCESS;
```

If existing ILM policies conflict with a new policy that you want to add, you will need to disable or delete the legacy policy. You can disable or delete ILM policies for ADO as shown in the following examples:

```
ALTER TABLE sales MODIFY PARTITION sales_q1_2002
    ILM DISABLE POLICY P2;
ALTER TABLE sales MODIFY PARTITION sales_q1_2002
    ILM DELETE POLICY P2;
```

## Move a datafile online

It is now possible in 12c to use the ALTER DATABASE MOVE DATAFILE SQL statement to rename or relocate a data file while the database is open and users are accessing it. When a data file is renamed or relocated, the pointers in the database control files that reference it are changed. At the same time, the files are also physically renamed or relocated in the operating system.

If there is already a file at the same name and location as the destination specified by the ALTER DATABASE statement, the statement will fail with an error by default. However, if the REUSE keyword is specified in the statement, Oracle will overwrite it with the datafile being renamed or moved.

When a data file is renamed or relocated with the ALTER DATABASE MOVE DATAFILE statement, a copy of the data file is created during the operation. There must be adequate disk space for both the original data file and the copy for the statement to succeed. At the end of the operation, the original file is deleted by default. If the KEEP option is specified, then the original is not deleted at the end of the operation. However, the database will only use the data file in the new location after the operation is completed.

The following examples demonstrate renaming a datafile, moving a datafile, moving a datafile with REUSE, and moving a datafile with KEEP respectively:

```
ALTER DATABASE MOVE DATAFILE '/u01/oracle/ocpdb/user1.dbf'
  TO '/u01/oracle/ocpdb/user_ts1.dbf';

ALTER DATABASE MOVE DATAFILE '/u01/oracle/ocpdb/user_ts1.dbf'
  TO '/u02/oracle/ocpdb/user_ts1.dbf';

ALTER DATABASE MOVE DATAFILE '/u01/oracle/ocpdb/user_ts1.dbf'
  TO '/u02/oracle/ocpdb/user_ts1.dbf' REUSE;

ALTER DATABASE MOVE DATAFILE '/u01/oracle/ocpdb/user_ts1.dbf'
  TO '/u02/oracle/ocpdb/user_ts1.dbf' KEEP;
```

# In-Database Archiving and Valid-Time Temporal

## Differentiate between ILM and Valid-Time Temporal

Oracle's Information Lifecycle Management (ILM) toolset is designed to optimize the way in which the storage resources of a database are utilized. As a general rule, the faster a given type of storage is, the more expensive it is. The quantity of data stored in enterprise databases using Oracle is often too large to justify purchasing enough top-tier storage to contain the complete contents of the database. ILM is designed to improve the utilization of storage and the performance of a database by making it more feasible to have tiered levels (speeds) of storage options. Using capabilities in ILM, Oracle can automatically move data among the storage tiers based on how frequently it is accessed. Alternately, ILM can improve storage utilization by compressing data that is accessed infrequently. Whether ILM compresses or moves data – the purpose is to optimize storage resource utilization with minimal impact to database performance.

The new Temporal Validity capability of Oracle allows you to create a valid time dimension for each row of a table. The data for this is stored in two hidden columns in the table definition. When querying the table, rows will be displayed whether or not they are "temporally valid" unless the query includes a filter against these columns. Temporal Validity has no effect on storage usage or database performance. It is simply providing a new means for filtering data.

## Set and use Valid Time Temporal

The new Temporal Validity feature of Oracle 12c provides a method of defining a range of time for each row in a table when it has real-world validity. The date range that indicates when a row is valid can be set by users and applications. In terms of ILM, the valid time attributes signify when data is valid and when it is not. Using these attributes, a query can return only rows that are currently valid.

Concepts that are integral to valid time temporal modeling include:

- **Valid time** -- This is a user-defined representation of time. Examples of a valid time include project start and finish dates, and employee hire and termination dates.
- **Tables with valid-time semantics** -- These tables have one or more dimensions of user-defined time, each of which has a start and an end.
- **Valid-time flashback queries** -- This is the ability to do as-of and versions queries using a valid-time dimension.

A valid-time period requires a pair of date-time columns be specified in the table definition. The columns can be explicitly added to the table, or they can be created implicitly. A valid-time period can be added during the create table or alter table process. The following statement creates a skeletal employees table that has valid-time temporal columns to define the specific 90-day probation period for the employee. No date columns are explicitly created, but the PERIOD FOR clause will create the columns implicitly.

```
CREATE TABLE probationary_emps (
emp_id       NUMBER PRIMARY KEY,
first_name   VARCHAR2(20),
last_name    VARCHAR2(25),
PERIOD FOR emp_probation);
```

When the table is described, only the EMP_ID, FIRST_NAME, and LAST_NAME columns appear:

```
DESCRIBE probationary_emps
Name             Null?      Type
-------------- --------- --------------
EMP_ID           NOT NULL  NUMBER
FIRST_NAME                 VARCHAR2(20)
LAST_NAME                  VARCHAR2(25)
```

## Querying the USER_TAB_COLS table shows that three additional hidden columns were created in the table:

```
SELECT column_name, data_type, column_id AS CID,
       internal_column_id AS ICID, hidden_column AS HID
FROM user_tab_cols
WHERE table_name = 'PROBATIONARY_EMPS';
```

| COLUMN_NAME | DATA_TYPE | CID | ICID | HID |
|---|---|---|---|---|
| EMP_PROBATION_START | TIMESTAMP(6) WITH TIME ZONE | | 1 | YES |
| EMP_PROBATION_END | TIMESTAMP(6) WITH TIME ZONE | | 2 | YES |
| EMP_PROBATION | NUMBER | | 3 | YES |
| EMP_ID | NUMBER | 1 | 4 | NO |
| FIRST_NAME | VARCHAR2 | 2 | 5 | NO |
| LAST_NAME | VARCHAR2 | 3 | 6 | NO |

## The following INSERT statements populate the table with two rows, each of which has a probation start and end dates with a 90-day span:

```
INSERT INTO probationary_emps(emp_probation_start, emp_probation_end,
      emp_id, first_name, last_name)
  VALUES ('01-OCT-13 12.00.01 PM CET', '30-DEC-13 12.00.01 PM CET',
     1234, 'John', 'Doe');
INSERT INTO probationary_emps(emp_probation_start, emp_probation_end,
      emp_id, first_name, last_name)
  VALUES ('14-SEP-13 12.00.01 PM CET', '13-DEC-13 12.00.01 PM CET',
     5678, 'Fred', 'Rogers');

SELECT emp_id
FROM   probationary_emps;
    EMP_ID
----------
      1234
      5678
```

Querying the table with a where clause that uses the hidden date field to filter the rows returned works exactly as you would expect:

```
SELECT  emp_id
FROM    probationary_emps
WHERE   emp_probation_start < '20-SEP-13 12.00.01 PM CET'
AND     emp_probation_end > '20-SEP-13 12.00.01 PM CET';

    EMP_ID
----------
      5678
```

That functionality does not do anything beyond what could be accomplished by adding normal DATE columns to the table. A somewhat more interesting capability is provided by the DBMS_FLASHBACK_ARCHIVE PL/SQL package. It contains the ENABLE_AT_VALID_TIME procedure. This procedure can be used to set the valid time visibility as of a supplied time.

```
EXECUTE DBMS_FLASHBACK_ARCHIVE.enable_at_valid_time
        ('ASOF', '20-DEC-13 12.00.01 PM');

SELECT  emp_id
FROM    probationary_emps;

    EMP_ID
----------
      5678
```

It can be used to set the visibility of temporal data to what is valid data for the current session's time.

```
EXECUTE DBMS_FLASHBACK_ARCHIVE.enable_at_valid_time('CURRENT');
SELECT  emp_id
FROM    probationary_emps;

no rows selected
```

The procedure can be used to set the visibility of temporal data to the full table (the default):

```
EXECUTE DBMS_FLASHBACK_ARCHIVE.enable_at_valid_time('ALL');
```

## Use In-Database archiving

The In-Database Archiving feature allows rows to be kept in a production database, but be kept invisible from applications. The idea is to have this data available in order to meet data compliance requirements but minimize impact to the performance of production applications. The archived data can be compressed to help improve backup performance. To use In-Database Archiving for a table, it must have ROW ARCHIVAL enabled and the value of the hidden column ORA_ARCHIVE_STATE must be set to a non-zero value.

When the ROW ARCHIVAL VISIBILITY session parameter is set to ACTIVE, only those rows with a value of zero in the ORA_ARCHIVE_STATE column will be displayed. When the parameter is set to ALL, queries will return both archived and non-archived rows in the table. The following example demonstrates In-Database Archiving:

```
ALTER SESSION SET ROW ARCHIVAL VISIBILITY = ACTIVE;

CREATE TABLE archival_test
  (col1    NUMBERL,
   col2    VARCHAR2(20)) ROW ARCHIVAL;

INSERT INTO archival_test (col1, col2)
  VALUES (1, 'Record One');

INSERT INTO archival_test (col1, col2)
  VALUES (2, 'Record Two');

INSERT INTO archival_test (col1, col2)
  VALUES (3, 'Record Three');

INSERT INTO archival_test (col1, col2)
  VALUES (4, 'Record Four');

SELECT col1, col2, ora_archive_state
FROM   archival_test;

COL1   COL2          ORA_ARCHIVE_STATE
-----  ------------  ------------------
    1  Record One                     0
    2  Record Two                     0
    3  Record Three                   0
    4  Record Four                    0
```

```
UPDATE archival_test
SET    ora_archive_state = '5'
WHERE  col1 = 3;

SELECT employee_id, ORA_ARCHIVE_STATE FROM employees_indbarch;

SELECT col1, col2, ora_archive_state
FROM   archival_test;

COL1   COL2          ORA_ARCHIVE_STATE
-----  ------------  ------------------
   1   Record One                     0
   2   Record Two                     0
   4   Record Four                    0

ALTER SESSION SET ROW ARCHIVAL VISIBILITY = ALL;

SELECT employee_id, ORA_ARCHIVE_STATE FROM employees_indbarch;

COL1   COL2          ORA_ARCHIVE_STATE
-----  ------------  ------------------
   1   Record One                     0
   2   Record Two                     0
   3   Record Three                   5
   4   Record Four                    0
```

# Auditing

## Enable and configure Unified Audit Data Trail

In Oracle 11g, audit trails were recorded in multiple locations, making it difficult for auditors to use the information. The new unified audit trail in 12c consolidates audit information from multiple sources and makes this information available in a standard format in the UNIFIED_AUDIT_TRAIL data dictionary view. The unified audit trail is maintained in a read-only table in the AUDSYS schema in the SYSAUX tablespace. The data is available to SYS and to users who have been granted the AUDIT_ADMIN or AUDIT_VIEWER roles. The AUDIT_ADMIN role can view the data and create audit policies. The AUDIT_VIEWER role can query the views but not create or alter policies. In unified auditing, the audit trail combines the audit records from the following sources:

- Unified audit policies and AUDIT settings
- Fine-grained audit records from DBMS_FGA
- Oracle Database Real Application Security
- Oracle Recovery Manager
- Oracle Database Vault
- Oracle Label Security
- Oracle Data Mining
- Oracle Data Pump
- Oracle SQL*Loader Direct Load

Once configured, unified auditing is always enabled and does not depend on the initialization parameters used in previous releases. If the database is opened in READ-ONLY mode, audit records are written to new operating system files in the $ORACLE_BASE/audit/$ORACLE_SID directory. The V$OPTION view can be queried to determine whether a database has been migrated to use unified auditing:

```
SELECT value
FROM    v$option
WHERE   parameter = 'Unified Auditing';

PARAMETER           VALUE
----------------    ----------
Unified Auditing    TRUE
```

This output shows that unified auditing is enabled. If it were disabled, the query would return FALSE. For newly created 12c databases, mixed mode auditing is enabled by default through the predefined policy ORA_SECURECONFIG. Mixed-mode auditing enables both traditional (pre-12c auditing) and unified auditing. The traditional auditing capabilities are controlled by the AUDIT_TRAIL initialization parameter. When set to a value other than 'none' in 12c, the traditional audit trail will be populated with audit records and the unified audit trail will also be populated. Audit settings can be applied to individual PDBs or to the CDB as a whole, depending on the type of policy. In a Multitenant environment, each PDB, including the root, has own unified audit trail.

When a database from an older release is upgraded to 12c, it is necessary to manually migrate to unified auditing if you want to use this capability. Once unified auditing is enabled, traditional auditing is disabled. To start using unified auditing, at least one unified audit policy must be enabled. To stop using it, disable all unified audit policies. The predefined policy ORA_SECURECONFIG is initially enabled on new 12c databases. The settings for this policy are:

```
CREATE AUDIT POLICY ORA_SECURECONFIG
PRIVILEGES ALTER ANY TABLE, CREATE ANY TABLE, DROP ANY TABLE,
CREATE ANY PROCEDURE, DROP ANY PROCEDURE, ALTER ANY PROCEDURE,
GRANT ANY PRIVILEGE, GRANT ANY OBJECT PRIVILEGE, GRANT ANY ROLE,
AUDIT SYSTEM, CREATE EXTERNAL JOB, CREATE ANY JOB,
CREATE ANY LIBRARY,
EXEMPT ACCESS POLICY,
CREATE USER, DROP USER,
ALTER DATABASE, ALTER SYSTEM,
CREATE PUBLIC SYNONYM, DROP PUBLIC SYNONYM,
CREATE SQL TRANSLATION PROFILE, CREATE ANY SQL TRANSLATION PROFILE,
DROP ANY SQL TRANSLATION PROFILE, ALTER ANY SQL TRANSLATION PROFILE,
CREATE ANY SQL TRANSLATION PROFILE, DROP ANY SQL TRANSLATION PROFILE,
```

```
ALTER ANY SQL TRANSLATION PROFILE, TRANSLATE ANY SQL,
EXEMPT REDACTION POLICY,
PURGE DBA_RECYCLEBIN, LOGMINING,
ADMINISTER KEY MANAGEMENT
ACTIONS ALTER USER, CREATE ROLE, ALTER ROLE, DROP ROLE, SET ROLE,
CREATE PROFILE, ALTER PROFILE, DROP PROFILE,
CREATE DATABASE LINK, ALTER DATABASE LINK, DROP DATABASE LINK,
LOGON, LOGOFF, CREATE DIRECTORY, DROP DIRECTORY;
```

## Disabling Unified Auditing

When disabling unified auditing, you should first disable any unified audit policies that are currently enabled. This will prevent the database from going into mixed mode auditing once unified auditing is disabled.

- Log into the database instance as a user with the AUDIT_ADMIN role and query the POLICY_NAME and ENABLED_OPT columns of the AUDIT_UNIFIED_ENABLED_POLICIES data dictionary view. Execute the NOAUDIT POLICY statement to disable any policies that are enabled.
- Connect as user SYS with the SYSOPER privilege.
- Shut down the database.

```
SHUTDOWN IMMEDIATE
```

- From the command prompt, run the following commands:

```
cd $ORACLE_HOME/rdbms/lib
make -f ins_rdbms.mk uniaud_off ioracle
```

- From SQL*Plus, restart the database.

```
STARTUP
```

By default, audit records are written to system global area (SGA) queues and then periodically written to the AUDSYS schema audit table in the SYSAUX tablespace. Queueing the records rather than immediately writing them to disk significantly improves the performance of the audit trail processes. However, if there is an instance crash or a SHUTDOWN ABORT, the queued writes mean there is a chance that some audit records may be lost. If this is not acceptable, the audit trail can be set to immediately write audit records to the AUDSYS schema audit table. Be aware that on an active database that this setting may affect performance. In a multitenant database, this option can be set for individual PDBs. To set the write mode for unified audit trail records:

- Log in to SQL*Plus as a user who has been granted the AUDIT_ADMIN role.
- Set the AUDIT_TRAIL_MODE property of the DBMS_AUDIT_MGMT package, as follows:
  To use immediate-write mode, run the following procedure:

```
BEGIN
 DBMS_AUDIT_MGMT.SET_AUDIT_TRAIL_PROPERTY(
  DBMS_AUDIT_MGMT.AUDIT_TRAIL_UNIFIED,
  DBMS_AUDIT_MGMT.AUDIT_TRAIL_WRITE_MODE,
  DBMS_AUDIT_MGMT.AUDIT_TRAIL_IMMEDIATE_WRITE);
END;
```

To use queued-write mode, run the following procedure:

```
BEGIN
 DBMS_AUDIT_MGMT.SET_AUDIT_TRAIL_PROPERTY(
  DBMS_AUDIT_MGMT.AUDIT_TRAIL_UNIFIED,
  DBMS_AUDIT_MGMT.AUDIT_TRAIL_WRITE_MODE,
  DBMS_AUDIT_MGMT.AUDIT_TRAIL_QUEUED_WRITE);
END;
```

Any time that the database is not writable, including when the instance is started but the database is closed or when the database is open in read-only mode, audit records are written to external files in the $ORACLE_BASE/audit/$ORACLE_SID directory. The contents of these files can be loaded into the database by running the DBMS_AUDIT_MGMT.LOAD_UNIFIED_AUDIT_FILES procedure. The process to do this is:

- Log into the database instance as a user who has been granted the AUDIT_ADMIN role.
- Ensure that the database is open and writable.
- Run the DBMS_AUDIT_MGMT.LOAD_UNIFIED_AUDIT_FILES procedure.

```
EXEC DBMS_AUDIT_MGMT.LOAD_UNIFIED_AUDIT_FILES;
```

- The audit records are loaded into the AUDSYS schema audit table immediately, and then deleted from the $ORACLE_BASE/audit/$ORACLE_SID directory.


## Create and enable audit policies

A unified audit policy is a named group of audit settings that track a particular aspect of user behavior in the database. The CREATE AUDIT POLICY statement is used to create a unified audit policy. More than one audit policy can be in effect concurrently in a database. They can contain both system-wide and object-specific audit options. The AUDIT and NOAUDIT SQL statements enable and disable an audit policy respectively. The AUDIT statement can also be used to include or exclude specific users for the given policy. The AUDIT and NOAUDIT statements also enable you to audit application context values. The following types of activities can be audited:

- User accounts (including administrative users who log in with the SYSDBA administrative privilege), roles, and privileges.
- Object actions, such as dropping a table or a running a procedure
- Application context values
- Activities from Oracle Database Real Application Security, Oracle Recovery Manager, Oracle Data Mining, Oracle Data Pump, Oracle SQL*Loader direct path events, Oracle Database Vault, and Oracle Label Security


It is possible to have multiple policies enabled concurrently, but ideally the number of enabled policies should be limited. The unified audit policy syntax is flexible enough to allow one policy to cover a number of audit settings. The best practice is to group related options into a single policy rather than creating multiple policies. Having a small number of policies reduces the logon overhead associated with loading audit policy details into the session's UGA memory. The session's UGA memory consumption is also reduced and the internal audit check functionality is more efficient.

When a unified audit policy is generated with the CREATE AUDIT POLICY statement, Oracle Database stores it in a first class object that is owned by the SYS schema, rather than the schema of the user who created the policy. The basic syntax for the CREATE AUDIT POLICY statement is:

```
CREATE AUDIT POLICY policy_name
{ {privilege_audit_clause [action_audit_clause ] [role_audit_clause
]}
| { action_audit_clause [role_audit_clause ] }
| { role_audit_clause }
}
[WHEN audit_condition EVALUATE PER {STATEMENT|SESSION|INSTANCE}]
[CONTAINER = {CURRENT | ALL}];
```

The following statement creates a policy that would generate an audit trail any time a statement requiring the ALTER ANY TABLE or DROP ANY TABLE system privileges granted via the ocp_admin role was executed.

```
CREATE AUDIT POLICY change_table_pol
PRIVILEGES ALTER ANY TABLE, DROP ANY TABLE
ROLES ocp_admin;
```

Once the policy has been created, it must be enabled using the AUDIT statement with the POLICY clause. The policy can be applied to one or more users, or to all users with specified exclusions. It is also possible to designate whether an audit record is written when the audited action succeeds, fails, or regardless of whether the action succeeds.

Newly-created policies will not take effect until after the audited user's next connection to the database instance. If the audited users are logged in when a policy is enabled, the policy cannot collect audit data until the users log out and back in to the database. The AUDIT statement supports the following optional clauses:

- **BY** -- Used to apply the unified audit policy to one or more users.

  ```
  AUDIT POLICY change_table_pol BY ocpuser;
  ```

- **EXCEPT** -- Used to exclude users from the unified audit policy.

  ```
  AUDIT POLICY change_table_pol EXCEPT jtkirk, jlpicard;
  ```

- **WHENEVER SUCCESSFUL** -- Records only successful executions of the audited activity.

  ```
  AUDIT change_table_pol WHENEVER SUCCESSFUL;
  ```

- **WHENEVER NOT SUCCESSFUL** -- Records only failed executions of the audited activity.

  ```
  AUDIT change_table_pol WHENEVER NOT SUCCESSFUL;
  ```

Note the following:

- **WHENEVER** -- If the WHENEVER clause is omitted, the both failed and successful user activities are written to the audit trail.
- **BY/EXCEPT** -- A unified audit policy can be enabled with either the BY clause or the EXCEPT clause, but not both simultaneously.
- **AUDIT...BY** -- If multiple AUDIT statements are executed on the same unified audit policy with different BY users, all of the specified users are audited.
- **AUDIT...EXCEPT** -- If multiple AUDIT statements are executed on the same unified audit policy with different EXCEPT users, only the last exception user list is used.
- **COMMON policies** -- Common unified audit policies can only be enabled from the root and only for common users.
- **LOCAL policies** -- Local audit policies can only be enabled from the PDB to which it applies.

No unified audit policy is required in order to audit Oracle Recovery Manager events. The UNIFIED_AUDIT_TRAIL view has several fields with names that start with RMAN_ which record RMAN-related events automatically. The RMAN-specific columns in UNIFIED_AUDIT_TRAIL include:

- **RMAN_SESSION_RECID** -- Recovery Manager session identifier. Together with the RMAN_SESSION_STAMP column, this column uniquely identifies the Recovery Manager job.
- **RMAN_SESSION_STAMP** -- Timestamp for the session.
- **RMAN_OPERATION** -- The Recovery Manager operation executed by the job.
- **RMAN_OBJECT_TYPE** -- Type of objects involved in a Recovery Manager session.
- **RMAN_DEVICE_TYPE** -- Device associated with a Recovery Manager session.

# Privileges

## Use administrative privileges

There are some changes to system privileges in Oracle 12c. Most of them are intended to increase the security of the database by providing a better separation of duties. The principle of least privilege should always be used to grant users the minimum level of privileges required for them to perform their duties.

There are three new roles for database administrative activities, including backup and recovery, high availability, and key management. The new roles eliminate the need to grant the SYSDBA role for common day-to-day operations.

- **SYSBACKUP** -- This allows Recovery Manager (RMAN) users to connect to the target database and perform RMAN backup and recovery either from RMAN or SQL*Plus.
- **SYSDG** -- The SYSDG administrative privilege is used to perform Data Guard operations. This privilege can be used with either Data Guard Broker or the DGMGRL command-line interface. In order to connect to the database as SYSDG using a password, you must create a password file for it.
- **SYSKM** -- The SYSKM administrative privilege enables the SYSKM user to manage Transparent Data Encryption wallet operations. In order to connect to the database as SYSKM using a password, you must create a password file for it.

There is a new system privilege related to the DBA recycle bin. Prior to 12c, the SYSDBA privilege was required to perform a purge of the DBA recycle bin. The new privilege "PURGE DBA_RECYCLEBIN" allows users to perform the PURGE DBA_RECYCLEBIN' command without requiring the SYSDBA privilege.

The SELECT ANY DICTIONARY privilege no longer permits access to security sensitive data dictionary tables DEFAULT_PWD$, ENC$, LINK$, USER$, USER_HISTORY$, and XS$VERIFIERS. This change increases the default security of the database by not allowing access to a subset of data dictionary tables through the SELECT ANY DICTIONARY privilege.

The UNLIMITED TABLESPACE privilege is no longer included in the RESOURCE role starting in Oracle Database 12c. This change increases the default security of the database by eliminating the potential for database users and applications that have been granted the RESOURCE role to exceed their intended resource quotas for tablespaces

## Create, enable and use privilege analysis

Privilege analysis is part of the capabilities provided by Oracle Database Vault. It allows for the creation of a profile for a database user that will capture the list of system and object privileges used. The results can be used to analyze used privileges vs. granted privileges. Using that information, the number of granted privileges can be reduced to only those which the user requires to perform their duties. Privilege analysis helps improve database security by identifying unused or excessive privileges. It is possible to perform privilege analysis with or without having Database Vault configured and enabled.

It is possible to administer the privilege analysis functionality from either Enterprise Manager Cloud Control or the DBMS_PRIVILEGE_CAPTURE PL/SQL package. To utilize the functionality, you must be granted the CAPTURE_ADMIN role, which provides the EXECUTE privilege for the DBMS_PRIVILEGE_CAPTURE package and the SELECT privilege on the views containing the results. The DBMS_PRIVILEGE_CAPTURE package enables you to create, enable, disable, and drop privilege analysis policies. It also generates reports that show the privilege usage, accessible via data dictionary views. The general steps that you use to analyze privileges are:

- Define the privilege analysis policy.

```
BEGIN
  DBMS_PRIVILEGE_CAPTURE.CREATE_CAPTURE(
      name         => 'ocprep_dev_role_pol',
      description  => 'Captures ocprep_dev role use',
      type         => DBMS_PRIVILEGE_CAPTURE.G_ROLE,
      roles        => role_name_list('ocprep_dev');
END;
```

- Enable the privilege analysis policy.

```
EXEC DBMS_PRIVILEGE_CAPTURE.ENABLE_CAPTURE
('ocprep_dev_role_pol');
```

- Disable the privilege analysis policy's recording of privilege use.

```
EXEC DBMS_PRIVILEGE_CAPTURE.DISABLE_CAPTURE
('ocprep_dev_role_pol');
```

- Generate privilege analysis results.

```
EXEC DBMS_PRIVILEGE_CAPTURE.GENERATE_RESULT
('ocprep_dev_role_pol');
SELECT username, sys_priv, object_owner, object_name
FROM   dba_used_privs
WHERE  capture = 'ocprep_dev_role_pol';
```

- Optionally, drop the privilege analysis policy.

```
EXEC DBMS_PRIVILEGE_CAPTURE.DROP_CAPTURE
('ocprep_dev_role_pol');
```

Only one privilege analysis policy in the database can be enabled concurrently. The only exception is that a privilege analysis policy of type DBMS_PRIVILEGE_CAPTURE.G_DATABASE can be enabled concurrently with a privilege analysis of a different type. If a privilege analysis policy is enabled before a database shutdown, it will still be enabled when the database is restarted. The privilege analysis policy must be disabled before it is possible to generate a privilege analysis report. Once you have completed analyzing the results, you can drop the analysis policy. A policy must be disabled before it can be dropped. Dropping a privilege analysis policy also drops all the used and unused privilege records associated with this privilege analysis.

Some of the views associated with privilege analysis include the following. Refer to the Oracle Database Vault manual for the complete list:

- **DBA_PRIV_CAPTURES** -- Lists information about existing privilege analysis policies
- **DBA_USED_PRIVS** -- Lists the privileges that have been used for reported privilege analysis policies
- **DBA_UNUSED_PRIVS** -- Lists the privileges that have not been used for reported privilege analysis policies
- **DBA_USED_OBJPRIVS** -- Lists the object privileges that have been used for reported privilege analysis policies. It does not include the object grant paths.
- **DBA_UNUSED_OBJPRIVS** -- Lists the object privileges that have not been used for reported privilege analysis policies. It does not include the object privilege grant paths.
- **DBA_USED_SYSPRIVS** -- Lists the system privileges that have been used for reported privilege analysis policies. It does not include the system privilege grant paths.
- **DBA_UNUSED_SYSPRIVS** -- Lists the system privileges that have not been used for reported privilege analysis policies. It does not include the system privilege grant paths.

# Oracle Data Redaction

## Use and manage Oracle Data Redaction policies

Data Redaction provides runtime redaction of sensitive data being returned by SQL queries prior to being displayed by applications. This ensures that unauthorized users cannot view sensitive data. Oracle Data Redaction provides consistent redaction of database columns across application modules accessing the same database information. It allows you to redact column data by any of the following methods:

- **Full redaction** -- The entire contents of the column data is redacted. The redacted value returned to the querying application user depends on the data type of the column. Columns of the NUMBER data type are redacted with a zero (0), and character data types are redacted with a single space.
- **Partial redaction** -- Only a portion of the column data is redacted. For example, you can redact most of a credit card number with pound signs (#), except for the last 4 digits.
- **Regular expressions** -- Regular expressions can be used to look for patterns of data to redact. Designed for use with character data only, it is most applicable for data with varying character lengths.
- **Random redaction** -- The redacted data presented to the querying application user appears as randomly generated values each time it is displayed, depending on the data type of the column.
- **No redaction** -- The 'None' redaction type option enables you to test the internal operation of your redaction policies, with no effect on the results of queries against tables with policies defined on them.

Data Redaction policies define the way in which the data will be masked, including:

- What kind of redaction to perform (Full, Partial, Random, etc.)
- How the redaction should occur (e.g. for partial redaction, which portion of the data is redacted).
- When the redaction should take place (which users should see redacted vs. actual data).

EXECUTE privileges on the DBMS_REDACT PL/SQL package are required in order to create and manage an Oracle Data Redaction policy. The procedures in that package include the following:

- **DBMS_REDACT.ADD_POLICY** -- Adds a Data Redaction policy to a table or view
- **DBMS_REDACT.ALTER_POLICY** -- Modifies a Data Redaction policy
- **DBMS_REDACT.UPDATE_FULL_REDACTION_VALUES** -- Globally updates the full redaction value for a given data type. You must restart the database instance before the updated values can be used.
- **DBMS_REDACT.ENABLE_POLICY** -- Enables a Data Redaction policy
- **DBMS_REDACT.DISABLE_POLICY** -- Disables a Data Redaction policy
- **DBMS_REDACT.DROP_POLICY** -- Drops a Data Redaction policy

A full data redaction policy redacts the entire contents of a data column. By default, NUMBER data type columns are replaced with zero (0) and character data type columns are replaced with a single space. The UPDATE_FULL_REDACTION_VALUES procedure of the DBMS_REDACT package can be used to modify one or both of these defaults. The following example shows how to use full redaction for all the values in the TRGT.CUST_DATA table CC_NUM column. The expression parameter applies the policy to any user querying the table, except for users who have been granted the EXEMPT REDACTION POLICY system privilege. SYS and SYSTEM automatically have the EXEMPT REDACTION POLICY system privilege. This means that both accounts can always bypass any existing Oracle Data Redaction policies and be able to view data from tables or views with Data Redaction policies.

Redaction policies created on table or view will apply to any views that are created on this target, including materialized views. The redaction policy will continue to be in effect throughout the length of a view chain (a view based on another view) created on the target. However, if another redaction policy is created for one of the dependent views, then for any columns in that view and its dependant views, the new policy will take precedence.

```
BEGIN
  DBMS_REDACT.ADD_POLICY(
    object_schema => 'trgt',
    object_name   => 'cust_data',
    column_name   => 'cc_num',
    policy_name   => 'redact_cc_num',
    function_type => DBMS_REDACT.FULL,
    expression    => '1=1');
END;
```

When you create any Oracle Data Redaction policy, the expression parameter in the DBMS_REDACT.ADD_POLICY procedure specifies the conditions in which the policy applies. It defines a Boolean expression that must evaluate to TRUE for the policy to be applied. It must be based on one of the following functions:

- **SYS_CONTEXT** -- This must be specified with a valid namespace. The default namespace for SYS_CONTEXT is USERENV. This includes values such as SESSION_USER and CLIENT_IDENTIFIER.
- **Application Express function** -- It is possible to use either the V or NV wrappers (for the APEX_UTIL.GET_SESSION_STATE and APEX_UTIL.GET_NUMERIC_SESSION_STATE functions respectively) as part of the expression.

The expression must follow these guidelines:

- Use only the following operators: =, !=, >, <, >=, <=
- Comparisons with NULL must be used with care. The expression must evaluate to TRUE and most comparisons with NULL tend to return FALSE.
- User-created functions in the expression parameter are not permitted.

Some examples of applying a redaction policy using the expression parameter include:

- **User Environment** -- The following example applies a Data Redaction policy based on the session user name:

```
expression => 'SYS_CONTEXT(''USERENV'',''SESSION_USER'') =
''OCPREP'''
```

- **Role** -- It is possible to enable or disable a policy using the SYS_SESSION_ROLES namespace based on a role. The value of the attribute is TRUE if the specified role is enabled for the querying application user and FALSE if the role is not enabled. The following example sets the policy to show the actual data to any application user who has the OCP_ADMIN role enabled, but redact the data for all of the other application users.

```
expression =>
'SYS_CONTEXT(''SYS_SESSION_ROLES'',''OCP_ADMIN'') =
''FALSE'''
```

- **No Filtering** -- The policy can be applied irrespective of the context to any user, with no filtering (minus SYS and users who have the EXEMPT REDACTION POLICY privilege). The following example applies the policy to any user (with the aforementioned exception)
```
expression => '1=1'
```

Granting trusted users the EXEMPT REDACTION POLICY system privilege exempts them from all Data Redaction policies. The person who creates a Data Redaction policy is not exempt from it unless the person is user SYS or has EXEMPT REDACTION POLICY privilege. The EXEMPT REDACTION POLICY system privilege is included in the DBA role. However, the privilege must be granted explicitly to users because it is not included in the WITH ADMIN OPTION for DBA role grants.

When using partial data redaction, only a portion of the column data is redacted. A social security number might have all but the last four digits replaced with an asterisk for example (***-**-1234). It is possible to create policies for columns that use character, number, or date-time data types. For policies that redact character data types, there are a number of pre-defined character redaction shortcuts available. Some of the available shortcuts include:

- **DBMS_REDACT.REDACT_US_SSN_F5** -- Redacts the first 5 numbers of Social Security numbers when the column is a VARCHAR2 data type. For example, the number 987-65-4320 becomes XXX-XX-4320.
- **DBMS_REDACT.REDACT_US_SSN_L4** -- Redacts the last 4 numbers of Social Security numbers when the column is a VARCHAR2 data type. For example, the number 987-65-4320 becomes 987-65-XXXX.
- **DBMS_REDACT.REDACT_US_SSN_ENTIRE** -- Redacts the entire Social Security number when the column is a VARCHAR2 data type. For example, the number 987-65-4320 becomes XXX-XX-XXXX.
- **DBMS_REDACT.REDACT_ZIP_CODE** -- Redacts a 5-digit postal code when the column is a VARCHAR2 data type. For example, 95476 becomes XXXXX.
- **DBMS_REDACT.REDACT_DATE_MILLENNIUM** -- Redacts dates that are in the DD-MON-YY format to 01-JAN-00 (January 1, 2000).
- **DBMS_REDACT.REDACT_DATE_EPOCH** -- Redacts all dates to 01-JAN-70.

The following example shows how Social Security numbers in a VARCHAR2 data type column and can be redacted using the REDACT_US_SSN_L4 shortcut.

```
BEGIN
  DBMS_REDACT.ADD_POLICY(
    object_schema       => 'trgt',
    object_name         => 'cust_data',
    column_name         => 'ssn',
    policy_name         => 'redact_cust_ssns',
    function_type       => DBMS_REDACT.PARTIAL,
    function_parameters => DBMS_REDACT.REDACT_US_SSN_L4,
    expression          => '1=1',
    policy_description  => 'Partially redacts last 4 numbers in SS
numbers');
END;
```

# RMAN and Flashback Data Archive

## Use RMAN enhancements

There are a number of enhancements that have been made to RMAN with the 12c release of Oracle.

### Table-Level Recovery from Backups

This may well be my favorite of the new features. It is now possible in RMAN to restore and recover a table or set of tables from existing backups using the new RECOVER TABLE option. Prior to this option, recovering individual tables using RMAN backups was a very labor-intensive process. It was necessary to restore and recover the required tablespaces to a separate disk location, export the desired tables and then import them to the original database. In my own production systems, I have always included regular full-database exports as part of the backup strategy to make it easier to recover individual tables if required.

### RMAN Command-Line Interface

The RMAN command-line interface has been enhanced to allow SQL commands to be issued without preceding the command with the SQL keyword. For the handful of commands that exist in both RMAN and SQL with different uses, it is still possible to specify the SQL keyword in order to eliminate ambiguity. It is also possible to use the DESCRIBE command on tables and views from the RMAN command-line.

## Active Database Duplication

Active DUPLICATE is a network-enabled restore method that is run on the auxiliary database to clone the source database. The auxiliary instance connects to the target instance and retrieves the backup sets over the network. This is very different from the image copy-based approach that was run on the source database in previous releases. The new method reduces the processing load on the target instance. It is possible to use unused block compression during the duplication process to reduce the size of backups being transported. Active DUPLICATE supports the section size option to divide data files into subsections. The sections are then restored in parallel across multiple channels on the auxiliary database.

## NOOPEN option for DUPLICATE

The new NOOPEN option of the DUPLICATE command disables automatic opening of a recovered clone database. This allows you to perform any database setting changes before opening the database. This feature is useful scenarios where the database must not be open with RESETLOGS prior to running upgrade scripts.

```
DUPLICATE TARGET DATABASE
TO newdb
FROM ACTIVE DATABASE
NOOPEN;
```

## Multisection Image Copies

Image copies can be taken with the SECTION SIZE option to divide data files into subsections that can be backed up in parallel across multiple channels. This feature reduces image copy creation time for large data files.

```
BACKUP
AS COPY
SECTION SIZE 200M
DATABASE;
```

## Multisection Incremental Backups

Incremental backups can be taken with the SECTION SIZE option to divide data files into subsections that can be backed up in parallel across multiple channels. This reduces the incremental backup time for large data files.

```
BACKUP
INCREMENTAL LEVEL 1
SECTION SIZE 200M
DATAFILE '/oradata/datafiles/users_01.dbf';
```

## Storage Snapshot Optimization

This feature makes it possible to use third-party technologies to take a storage snapshot of your database without putting the database in BACKUP mode. Backup mode can induce additional system and I/O overhead due to the need to write whole block images into redo. With the new capability, a third-party storage snapshot that meets the following requirements can be taken without requiring the database to be placed in backup mode:

- Database is crash-consistent at the point of the snapshot.
- Write ordering is preserved for each file within a snapshot.
- Snapshot stores the time at which a snapshot is completed.

The SNAPSHOT TIME keyword has been introduced to the RECOVER command to allow you to recover a snapshot to a consistent point, without any additional manual procedures for point-in-time recovery needs. The snapshot can then be used to recover all or part of the database.

# Implement the new features in Flashback Data Archive

There are a few new features in Oracle's Flashback Data Archive (FDA).
They include:

- **User-context tracking** -- The user context is now part of the metadata information included when tracking transactions. With this, it is much easier to determine which user made which changes to a table. The SET_CONTEXT_LEVEL procedure of the DBMS_FLASHBACK_ARCHIVE package is used to set the user context level and the GET_SYS_CONTEXT to access the context information. The following example sets the context to TYPICAL, which includes user ID, global user ID and the hostname:

```
BEGIN
DBMS_FLASHBACK_ARCHIVE.SET_CONTEXT_LEVEL ('TYPICAL');
END;
```

- **Database hardening** -- A set of tables can be associated in an "application". It is then possible to enable Flashback Data Archive on the entire set of tables with a single command. It is also possible to lock the full set of tables with a single command, which will prevent DML operations on them until they are unlocked. This feature makes it easier to track and protect groups of related security-sensitive tables. The REGISTER_APPLICATION procedure of the DBMS_FLASHBACK_ARCHIVE package is used to register an application for database hardening. For more details, refer to the Oracle Database PL/SQL Packages and Types Reference.

- **Import and export of history** -- It is possible to use the DBMS_FLASHBACK_ARCHIVE procedures to create a temporary history table. The temporary table can be loaded with desired history data using a variety of methods, including Data Pump. Once filled, the data in the temporary table can then be imported into a designated history table. Support is also included for importing user-generated history if a mechanism such as triggers has been maintaining history data. For more details on the DBMS_FLASHBACK_ARCHIVE package, refer to the Oracle Database PL/SQL Packages and Types Reference.

# Real-Time Database Operation Monitoring

## Implement real-time database operation monitoring

A database operation can be any group of related database tasks as defined by end users or an application. Examples of operations include ETL processing, a batch jobs, or a multiple SQL-statement transaction. Database operations are either simple or composite.

- **Simple** -- A single SQL statement or PL/SQL procedure or function.
- **Composite** -- Activity between two points in time in a database session, with each session defining its own beginning and end points. A session can participate in at most one composite database operation at a time.

When Real-Time SQL Monitoring was introduced in Oracle Database 11g, it supported only simple operations. With 12c, Real-Time Database Operations provides the ability to monitor composite operations. Oracle automatically monitors parallel queries, DML, and DDL statements as soon as execution begins. By default, Real-Time SQL Monitoring automatically starts when a SQL statement runs in parallel, or when it has consumed at least 5 seconds of CPU or I/O time in a single execution.

The data from Real-Time SQL Monitoring can be accessed from the Enterprise Manager Cloud Control Monitored SQL Executions page, via data dictionary views, or through the DBMS_MONITOR package. The Monitored SQL Executions page in EM Cloud Control is available from the Performance menu. This page summarizes the activity for monitored statements and is the recommended method for using Real-Time SQL Monitoring. You can use it to drill down and obtain additional details about particular statements.

The data dictionary views for Real-Time SQL monitoring include:

- **V$SQL_MONITOR** -- This view contains global, high-level information about the top SQL statements in a database operation. Each monitored SQL statement has an entry in this view. Each row contains a SQL statement whose statistics are accumulated from multiple sessions and all of its executions in the operation. The primary key is the combination of the columns DBOP_NAME, DBOP_EXEC_ID, and SQL_ID.

- **V$SQL_MONITOR_SESSTAT** -- This view contains the statistics for all sessions involved in the database operation. Most of the statistics are cumulative. The database stores the statistics in XML format instead of using each column for each statistic. This view is primarily intended for the report generator.

- **V$SQL_PLAN_MONITOR** -- This view contains monitoring statistics for each step in the execution plan of the monitored SQL statement. The database updates statistics in V$SQL_PLAN_MONITOR every second while the SQL statement is executing. Multiple entries exist in V$SQL_PLAN_MONITOR for every monitored SQL statement. Each entry corresponds to a step in the execution plan of the statement.

The DBMS_SQL_MONITOR package allows you to define the beginning and ending of a database operation, and generate a report of the database operations. The functions in this package include:

- **REPORT_SQL_MONITOR** -- This function accepts several input parameters to specify the execution, the level of detail in the report, and the report type. If no parameters are specified, then the function generates a text report for the last execution that was monitored.
- **BEGIN_OPERATION** -- This function associates a session with a database operation.

- **END_OPERATION** -- This procedure disassociates a session from the specified database operation execution.

```
DBMS_MONITOR.BEGIN_OPERATION(
    dbop_name IN VARCHAR2,
    dbop_eid IN NUMBER := NULL,
    force_tracking IN VARCHAR2 := NO_FORCE_TRACKING,
    attribute_list IN VARCHAR2 := NULL)
RETURN NUMBER;
```

The BEGIN_OPERATION function is used to begin a composite data operation. It accepts the following parameters:

- **dbop_name** -- Name of operation
- **dbpop_eid** -- Unique number to distinguish the execution provided by the user
- **force_tracking** -- FORCE_TRACKING forces the composite database operation to be tracked when the operation starts. By default, NO_FORCE_TRACKING is in effect, which means that the operation is tracked only when it is sufficiently expensive.
- **attribute_list** -- List of the user input attributes in the form of a comma separated name-value pair (for example, table_name=emp, operation=load)

SQL monitoring is enabled by default when the initialization parameter STATISTICS_LEVEL is set to either TYPICAL or ALL. Oracle will begin monitoring long running queries automatically. The initialization parameter CONTROL_MANAGEMENT_PACK_ACCESS must also be set to DIAGNOSTIC+TUNING (the default) for SQL monitoring to be used.

It is possible to use hints to enable or disable monitoring of specific SQL statements. The MONITOR hint enables monitoring, whereas the NO_MONITOR hint disables monitoring. The first statement below enables SQL Monitoring explicitly and the second disables it:

```
SELECT /*+ MONITOR */ first_name, last_name, email
FROM   employees;


SELECT /*+ NO_MONITOR */ first_name, last_name, email
FROM   employees;
```

You can create a database operation by explicitly defining its beginning and end points using the DBMS_SQL_ONITOR package. A database operation is started with the BEGIN_OPERATION function and ended with the END_OPERATION procedure.

To create a database operation:

- Start SQL*Plus and connect as a user with the appropriate privileges.
- Define a variable to hold the execution ID.

  ```
  var    opid   NUMBER
  ```

- Begin the database operation.

  ```
  EXEC :opid := DBMS_SQL_MONITOR.BEGIN_OPERATION('rtsm_op');
  ```

- Run the queries in the operation.
  ```
  SELECT count(*) FROM hr.employees;

  SELECT COUNT(*) FROM hr.departments;
  ```

- End the database operation.

  ```
  EXEC DBMS_SQL_MONITOR.END_OPERATION('rtsm_op', :opid);
  ```

- Confirm that the database operation completed.

  ```
  SELECT dbop_name, status
  FROM   v$sql_monitor
  WHERE  dbop_name = 'rtsm_op';
  DBOP_NAME  STATUS
  ---------- ---------
  rtsm_op    DONE
  ```

# SQL Tuning

## Use Adaptive Execution Plans

The new Adaptive Query Optimization in 12c enables the optimizer to alter execution plans at run-time and also to discover additional information that can generate better statistics. There are two distinct aspects in Adaptive Query Optimization

- **Adaptive plans** -- This capability focuses on improving the initial execution of a query at run-time.
- **Adaptive statistics** -- This feature is intended to provide additional statistics in order to improve subsequent executions of a query.

### Adaptive Plans

Adaptive plans allow the optimizer to make the final plan decision for a SQL statement while it is being executed. The plan chosen by the optimizer prior to execution is instrumented with statistics collectors. The optimizer can detect at run-time if its cardinality estimates differ significantly from the actual number of rows. If so, the plan or a portion of it can be automatically adapted in mid-execution.

The optimizer can predetermine multiple potential subplans for portions of the plan so that it can decide on the method to be used on the fly. During execution of the statement, the statistics collector will monitor and buffer rows coming from a portion of the plan. Based on the data collected, the optimizer will make the final decision about which subplan to use. Once the optimizer has chosen the final plan, the statistics collector stops collecting statistics and buffering rows, and simply passes the rows through. On subsequent executions of the child cursor, the optimizer will disable buffering and choose the same final plan.

When an execution plan is altered by Adaptive Query Optimization, the results of the EXPLAIN PLAN command will be different from that of the DBMS_XPLAN.DISPLAY_CURSOR function. The explain plan command will show only the initial or default plan chosen by the optimizer. The results of the DBMS_XPLAN.DISPLAY_CURSOR function will be the final plan used by the query.

It is possible to see all of the operations in an adaptive plan, including the positions of the statistics collectors using the DBMS_XPLAN functions. Adding the format parameter '+adaptive' will result in an additional notation (-) in the id column of the plan. This indicates operations in the plan that were not used (inactive). The SQL Monitor tool in Oracle Enterprise Manager always shows the full adaptive plan but does not indicate which operations in the plan are inactive.

The V$SQL view has a new column (IS_RESOLVED_ADAPTIVE_PLAN) that indicates if a SQL statement has an adaptive plan and if that plan has been fully resolved or not. If the column value is set to 'Y', the plan adaptive and a final plan has been selected. If the column value is 'N', the plan selected is adaptive but the final plan has not yet been decided on. The column value will be NULL for non-adaptive plans.

If the initialization parameter OPTIMIZER_ADAPTIVE_REPORTING_ONLY is set to TRUE (the default value is FALSE), information needed to enable adaptive join methods will be gathered, but no action is taken to change the plan. When set to TRUE, the default plan will always be used but information is collected on how the plan would have been adapted. This information can be viewed by using DBMS_XPLAN to display the plan using the additional format parameter '+report'.


**Adaptive Statistics**

The optimizer depends on statistics in order to create good execution plans. However, some query predicates are too complex to rely on base table statistics alone. When a SQL statement is being compiled, the optimizer determines whether or not a good execution plan can be generated with the available statistics. If not, dynamic sampling is used to compensate for missing or insufficient statistics. If one or more of the tables in the query does not have statistics, dynamic sampling will gather basic statistics on them. In Oracle Database 12c dynamic sampling has been enhanced to become dynamic statistics.

Dynamic statistics can determine more accurate cardinality estimates for not only single table accesses but also joins and group-by predicates. A new level, 11 has also been introduced for the initialization parameter OPTIMIZER_DYNAMIC_SAMPLING. When the parameter is set to this level, the optimizer can decide to use dynamic statistics for any SQL statement, even where all of the basic table statistics exist. The decision on whether to use dynamic statistics is based on the complexity of the predicates used, the existing base statistics, and the total execution time expected for the SQL statement. At level 11, dynamic sampling will almost certainly occur more often and extend parse times. To minimize the performance impact, the results of the dynamic sampling queries will be persisted in the cache for other SQL statements to share.

Automatic reoptimization is designed to improve execution plans after the initial execution. At the end of the first execution of a SQL statement, the optimizer determines whether the execution information differs significantly from the original estimates. If so, the optimizer looks for a replacement plan for the next execution. Automatic reoptimization is iterative, the optimizer can reoptimize a query multiple times, each time learning more and further improving the plan. Oracle Database 12c supports multiple forms of reoptimization.

- **Statistics feedback** -- Formally known as cardinality feedback, this is designed to improve plans for queries that have cardinality misestimates. When used the optimizer compares its original cardinality estimates for a SQL statement to the actual cardinalities observed during execution. If they differ significantly the correct estimates are stored for subsequent use. It will also create a SQL plan directive so other SQL statements can benefit from the information gathered during this initial execution.

- **Performance Feedback** -- This helps to improve the degree of parallelism used for repeated SQL statements when Automatic Degree of Parallelism (AutoDOP) is enabled in adaptive mode. During the first execution of a SQL statement, the optimizer determines what parallel degree (if any) should be used. At the end of the initial execution, the parallel degree used is compared to the parallel degree computed based on the actual performance statistics gathered during the execution of the statement. If the two vary significantly, the statement is marked for reoptimization and the statistics are stored to help compute a more appropriate DOP on subsequent executions.

- **SQL plan directives** -- A SQL plan directive is additional information that the optimizer uses to generate a more optimal execution plan. They are created on query expressions rather than at a statement or object level so that they can be applied to multiple SQL statements. Multiple SQL plan directives can be used for a single SQL statement. SQL plan directives are maintained automatically and stored in the SYSAUX tablespace. Any SQL plan directive that is not used after 53 weeks will be automatically purged. They can be monitored using the views DBA_SQL_PLAN_DIRECTIVES and DBA_SQL_PLAN_DIR_OBJECTS.

## Use enhanced features of statistics gathering

There were two enhancements made to the process of gathering incremental statistics. Incremental statistics are relevant when gathering statistics on partitioned tables. For partitioned tables, Oracle must gather statistics at both the table and partition levels. It is possible for Oracle to derive the global level statistics by aggregating the partition level statistics, and eliminate the need to scan the entire table to produce global statistics.

Prior to 12c, if incremental statistics were enabled on a table and a single row changed in a partition, the statistics for it were considered stale. They could not be used to generate global level statistics until they were re-gathered. A new preference called INCREMENTAL_STALENESS allows the

DBA to determine when partition statistics will be marked as stale. It is set to NULL by default, which uses the legacy definition of staleness. Alternately, the parameter can be set to the following values:

- **USE_STALE_PERCENT** -- The partition level statistics will not be considered stale until the percentage of rows changed is greater than the value of the preference STALE_PERCENTAGE (10% by default).
- **USE_LOCKED_STATS** -- If statistics on a partition are locked, they will be used to generate global level statistics regardless of how many rows have changed in that partition since statistics were last gathered.

The second enhancement to incremental statistics involves the exchange partition capability. The exchange partition command allows data from a non-partitioned table to be swapped into a specified partition of a partitioned table. Data is not physically moved by the command -- it simply updates the data dictionary to exchange a pointer from the partition to the table and vice versa. Prior to 12c, it was not possible to generate the statistics on the non-partitioned table required to support incremental statistics. The statistics had to be gathered on the partition after the exchange. In 12c, the statistics (synopsis) can be created on the non-partitioned table prior to the exchange operation. After the exchange, this data can immediately be used to maintain incremental global statistics. The new DBMS_STATS table preference INCREMENTAL_LEVEL can be used to identify a non-partitioned table that will be used in partition exchange. When INCREMENTAL_LEVEL is set to TABLE (the default is PARTITION), Oracle will automatically create a synopsis for the table when statistics are gathered. This synopsis will then become the partition level synopsis after the exchange.

## Concurrent Statistics

When the global statistics gathering preference CONCURRENT is set, the Oracle Job Scheduler and Advanced Queuing components create and manage one statistics gathering job per object (tables and/or partitions) concurrently. In 12c, the process of gathering statistics concurrently has been improved to make better use of each scheduler job. For small (or empty) tables, partitions, or sub-partitions, the database can automatically batch the object with other small objects into a single job to reduce overhead. It is also now possible to perform concurrent statistics gathering via the nightly statistics gathering job by setting the preference CONCURRENT to ALL or AUTOMATIC.

## Automatic column group detection

When multiple columns from the same table are used in filter predicates, join conditions, or group-by keys, extended statistics on those column groups can improve the accuracy of cardinality estimates by the Optimizer. However, it is often difficult to determine which column groups to create extended statistics for. The Auto Column Group detection can automatically derive this information based on a given workload. Auto Column Group detection is a three step process:

- **Seed column usage** -- Oracle must observe a representative workload, in order to determine the appropriate column groups. The workload can be provided via a SQL Tuning Set or by monitoring a running system. The DBMS_STATS.SEED_COL_USAGE procedure is used to indicate the workload and to tell Oracle how long to observe it.
- **Create the column groups** -- Calling the DBMS_STATS.CREATE_EXTENDED_STATS function for the relevant table(s), will create the necessary column groups based on the usage information captured. Once the extended statistics have been created, they will be automatically maintained whenever statistics are gathered on the table. It is also possible to create column groups manually by specifying the group as the third

argument in the DBMS_STATS.CREATE_EXTENDED_STATS function.

- **Regather statistics** -- The final step is to regather statistics on the affected tables.

## Use Adaptive SQL Plan Management

The new adaptive SQL plan management feature in 12c means that DBAs no longer have to manually run the verification or evolve process for non-accepted plans. The SPM Evolve Advisor runs a verification process (SYS_AUTO_SPM_EVOLVE_TASK) for all SQL statements that have non-accepted plans during the nightly maintenance window when automatic SQL tuning is in COMPREHENSIVE mode. If the verification process determines that the non-accepted plan performs sufficiently better than the existing accepted plan (or plans) in the SQL plan baseline, the plan will be automatically accepted. The task can accept more than one plan for a given SQL statement. A persistent report is generated that details how the new plan performs in comparison to the existing plans. The evolution task can also be run manually using the DBMS_SPM package.

The Automatic SPM Evolve Advisor task does not have a separate scheduler client. A single client controls both Automatic SQL Tuning Advisor and Automatic SPM Evolve Advisor. The same task enables or disables both advisors. The task can be enabled through Enterprise manager or via the DBMS_AUTO_TASK_ADMIN PL/SQL package. The steps to enable the task using DBMS_AUTO_TASK_ADMIN follow:

- Connect SQL*Plus to the database with administrator privileges and execute the following PL/SQL block:

```
BEGIN
DBMS_AUTO_TASK_ADMIN.ENABLE (
    client_name  => 'sql tuning advisor',
    operation    => NULL,
    window_name  => NULL
   );
END;
```

- Query the data dictionary to confirm the change.

```
SELECT client_name, status
FROM   dba_autotask_client
WHERE  client_name = 'sql tuning advisor';

CLIENT_NAME          STATUS
-------------------- --------
sql tuning advisor   ENABLED
```

Executing the DBMS_AUTO_TASK_ADMIN.DISABLE procedure with the same parameters will disable the task. The DBMS_SPM package allows for configuration of automatic plan evolution. Reference the Oracle Database SQL Tuning Guide for details on how to do this.

It is recommended that the SQL Plan Management Evolve task be set to run automatically. However, it is possible use PL/SQL or Cloud Control to manually evolve an unaccepted plan. A manual evolution will allow you to determine is the new plan performs better than any accepted plan currently in the baseline. The following list contains the most relevant DBMS_SPM procedures and functions for managing plan evolution.

- **ACCEPT_SQL_PLAN_BASELINE** -- This function accepts one recommendation to evolve a single plan into a SQL plan baseline.
- **CREATE_EVOLVE_TASK** -- This function creates an advisor task to prepare the plan evolution of one or more plans for a specified SQL statement. The input parameters can be a SQL handle, plan name or a list of plan names, time limit, task name, and description.
- **EXECUTE_EVOLVE_TASK** -- This function executes an evolution task. The input parameters can be the task name, execution name, and execution description. If not specified, the advisor generates the name, which is returned by the function.
- **IMPLEMENT_EVOLVE_TASK** -- This function implements all recommendations for an evolve task.

- **REPORT_EVOLVE_TASK** -- This function displays the results of an evolve task as a CLOB. Input parameters include the task name and section of the report to include.
- **SET_EVOLVE_TASK_PARAMETER** -- This function updates the value of an evolve task parameter. In this release, the only valid parameter is TIME_LIMIT.

Normally, the steps to manually evolve a SQL plan evolution tasks occur in the following sequence:

- Create an evolve task
- Optionally, set evolve task parameters
- Execute the evolve task
- Implement the recommendations in the task
- Report on the task outcome

# Emergency Monitoring, Real-Time ADDM, Compare Period ADDM, and Active Session History (ASH) Analytics

## Perform emergency monitoring and real-time ADDM

The Emergency Monitoring feature of Enterprise Manager Cloud Control allows a DBA to connect to an unresponsive database. The connection is created via a proprietary mechanism and facilitates diagnosis of the performance problem when a normal mode connection is not possible.

On entering the Emergency Monitoring page, the agent will connect directly to the SGA. The agent bypasses the SQL retrieval layer and collects data directly from the SGA to get performance statistics. The page displays collected ASH data and top blocking sessions in the Hang Analysis table refreshed in real-time. The screen enables administrators to identify blocking sessions and kill these blockers with a click of a button. The Emergency Monitoring page is accessed from the Performance Menu in the home page of EM Cloud Control.

### Real-Time ADDM

Real-Time ADDM was originally introduced with Oracle Enterprise Manager Cloud Control 12c and much of the functionality is also available in Enterprise manager Express (EM Express has no equivalent of the diagnostic connection). Real-Time ADDM is designed to assist in the analysis and resolution of problems that cause unresponsive or hung databases. Traditionally performance problems that caused this would require the database to be restarted.

Real-Time ADDM analyzes the current performance of the database via a set of predefined criteria. If any problems are detected, Real-Time ADDM suggests methods for resolving any issues it identifies without restarting the database. Depending on the database state, Real-Time ADDM will use one of two connection modes to the database:

- **Normal connection** -- Real-Time ADDM performs a normal JDBC connection to the database. This mode is intended to perform extensive performance analysis of the database when some connectivity is available.
- **Diagnostic connection** -- This is a latch-less connection to the database that is intended for extreme hang situations when a normal JDBC connection is not possible.

Real-Time ADDM performs a similar type of diagnosis as conventional ADDM to analyze performance, but uses different data. Conventional ADDM makes use of the data from AWR snapshots to perform its diagnosis. Real-Time ADDM makes use of ASH recent activity from SGA data in lieu of AWR snapshots. Real-Time ADDM runs automatically and uses in-memory data to locate performance spikes in the database. If a performance problem is detected, an analysis is triggered automatically. The scans are executed every three seconds by the manageability monitor process (MMON) to obtain performance statistics without lock or latch. MMON will analyze the statistics and trigger a Real-Time ADDM analysis if any of the following issues are detected.

- **High load** -- Average active sessions are greater than 3 times the number of CPU cores
- **I/O bound** -- I/O impact on active sessions based on single block read performance
- **CPU bound** -- Active sessions are greater than 10% of total load and CPU utilization is greater than 50%
- **Over-allocated memory** -- Memory allocations are over 95% of physical memory
- **Interconnect bound** -- Based on single block interconnect transfer time
- **Session limit** -- Session limit is close to 100%
- **Process limit** -- Process limit is close to 100%
- **Hung session** -- Hung sessions are greater than 10% of total sessions

- **Deadlock detected** -- Any deadlock is detected

The MMON slave process will then store the ADDM report that was created in the AWR. The report metadata can be accessed via the DBA_HIST_REPORTS view. Real-Time ADDM employs several controls to ensure that the automatic triggers do not consume too many system resources:

- **Duration between reports** -- If a Real-Time ADDM report was created in the past 5 minutes by the automatic trigger, then no new reports will be generated.
- **Oracle RAC control** -- Automatic triggers are local to the database instance. For Oracle RAC, only one database instance can create a Real-Time ADDM report at a given time because a lock is required and a query is performed by the MMON slave process before the report is actually generated.
- **Repeated triggers** -- An automatic trigger for any issue must have an impact of 100% or higher than the previous report with the same triggering issue within the past 45 minutes.
- **Newly identified issues** -- If a new issue is found that was not previously detected within the past 45 minutes, a new report is generated regardless of the new active sessions load.

## Generate ADDM Compare Period

The Compare Period ADDM feature is used to compare the performance of the database server in two distinct time periods. This is often used to determine why the server is slower (or faster) at different points in time. The ADDM Compare Period functionality is part of Enterprise Manager Cloud Control 12c. It can analyze any Oracle database monitored by Cloud Control that is release 10.2.0.4 or later. The functionality requires exactly two periods to be selected:

- **Comparison Period** -- This is normally the period that exhibits a performance degradation. It is possible, though, to use Compare Period ADDM to determine why performance has improved.
- **Base Period** -- The base period represents a known period in which the database is functioning properly. The base period should be one in which the performance was acceptable, and the workload was as similar to the Comparison period.

The steps to initiate a report from the Compare Period ADDM are:

1. From the Performance menu of EM Cloud Control, select AWR, then Compare Period ADDM.
2. From the Run Compare Period ADDM page, specify the comparison and base periods to be used.
3. Click Run to display the Database Compare Period Report.
4. Examine the Compare Period ADDM report to analyze why the performance changed between the two periods.

The Compare Period ADDM Report contains four sections:

- **Overview** -- This section shows how comparable the two periods were. The value is based on the average resource consumption of the SQL statements common to both periods. When the value is 100%, the workload "signature" in both time periods is identical. If the value is 0%, the time periods have no items in common for the specific workload dimension.
- **Configuration** -- This section displays base period and comparison period values for various parameters categorized by instance, host, and database.
- **Findings** -- This section can display performance improvements or degradations. It can identify the major performance differences caused by system changes. It contains a Change Impact value that represents the scale of a change in performance from one time period to another. If the value is positive, an improvement has occurred, and if the value is negative, a regression has occurred.

- **Resources** -- The information displayed in this section provides a summary of the division of database time for both time periods. It provides the resource usage for CPU, memory, I/O, and interconnect on RAC installations.

# Diagnose performance issues using ASH enhancements

Conventional ADDM performs diagnosis from the data in AWR snapshots. When a performance problem is short-lived, ADDM may not report it because it is not considered significant enough in terms of its duration when compared to the interval between AWR snapshots. Snapshot data is not the ideal means for locating and diagnosing transient performance problems. In order to facilitate the identification performance problems that last for short durations, Oracle Database samples active sessions every second and stores the data collected in a circular buffer in the SGA. To keep the amount of data to a manageable level, only sessions that are waiting on an event that does not belong to the Idle wait class are sampled. This collected data is known as Active Session History (ASH). The data can be queried via the V$ACTIVE_SESSION_HISTORY view and rolled up in various dimensions into an ASH report, including the following:

- SQL identifier of a SQL statement
- Object number, file number, and block number
- Wait event identifier and parameters
- Session identifier and session serial number
- Module and action name
- Client identifier of the session
- Service hash identifier

It is possible to generate ASH reports using Oracle Enterprise Manager Cloud Control. To run ASH reports from EM Cloud Control:

- Access the Database Home page.
- From the Performance menu, select Performance Home.
- Log in to the database as a user with administrator privileges. The Performance page appears.
- Under Average Active Sessions, click Run ASH Report. The Run ASH Report page appears.
- Enter the date and time for the start and end of the time period when the transient performance problem occurred.
- Click Generate Report.

Once the report has been generated, the ASH report will appear under Report Results on the Run ASH Report page. The report can be used to identify the source of transient performance problems. An ASH report is divided into titled sections:

- **Top Events** -- Details the top wait events of the sampled session activity categorized by user, background, and priority.
- **Load Profile** -- Describes the load analyzed in the sampled session activity. The information in this section can be used to identify the service, client, or SQL command type that may be the cause of the transient performance problem.
- **Top SQL** -- Shows the top SQL statements in the sampled session activity. The high-load SQL statements identified here may be a contributing factor of the transient performance problem.
- **Top Sessions** -- Lists the sessions that were waiting for the wait event that accounted for the highest percentages of sampled session activity. This can help to identify the sessions that may be the cause of the performance problem.
- **Top DB Objects/Files/Latches** -- This section provides additional information about the most commonly-used database resources. The three subsections of this report list the top object, files, and latches that accounted for the highest percentages of sampled session activity.
- **Activity Over Time** -- This section is useful for longer time periods because it provides in-depth details about activities and workload profiles during the analysis period.

EM Cloud Control also contains a new ASH Analytics page that provides a graphical view of the ASH information. This allows for a more interactive method of analyzing the ASH data and provides several capabilities for manipulating the data being analyzed, including:

- Varying the size of the time period to be analyzed.
- Filtering the dimensions to be included
- Drilling down to a load map view that displays the various waits with the importance of each indicated by size.

# Resource Manager and Other Performance Enhancements

## Use Resource Manager for a CDB and PDB

The Resource Manager is used to manipulate how the system resources for an Oracle database are allocated among multiple competing workloads. Competing workloads are complex enough in an Oracle database that is <u>not</u> using the multitenant architecture. Resource management in a CDB becomes much more complex as resources are now being shared among multiple PDBs competing for system and CDB resources. Resource Manager works on two basic levels in a CDB environment:

- **CDB level** - It manages the workloads for multiple PDBs that are competing for resources. It is possible to specify how resources should be allocated among various PDBs, and limits can be set for specific PDBs.
- **PDB level** - Workloads within each PDB can be managed.

Resources are allocated in a two-step process:

- Each PDB is allocated a portion of the total system resources in the CDB.
- Within each specific PDB, the resources obtained in the first step are allocated among the connected sessions.

The Resource Manager allows administrators to perform the following:

- Specify that different PDBs should receive varying shares of the system resources based on the relative importance of each PDB.
- Limit the CPU usage of a particular PDB
- Limit the number of parallel execution servers that a particular PDB can use

- Limit the resource usage of different sessions connected to a single PDB
- Monitor the resource usage of PDBs

## Explain Multi-process Multi-threaded Oracle architecture

The Oracle database uses a number of different processes to perform various tasks for the database. The PMON process has one set of jobs while SMON has another set, LGWR a third and so on. This is the multi-process architecture. If Oracle were a single process database, then there would simply be one gargantuan process that ran everything. The multi-process architecture makes Oracle more scalable, since only the processes that are needed for any given system are running (and using resources) for that instance.

Prior to Oracle 12c, under the Unix and Linux operating systems, each Oracle process required one operating system process. With this release, it is possible to have Oracle run in a multithreaded mode. When running in the multithreaded model, one operating system process can support multiple Oracle processes running as operating system threads within it.

The multithreaded mode is not enabled when a new 12c database is created. In order to enable this mode, the THREADED_EXECUTION parameter must be set to YES and the database restarted. When running in threaded mode, some background processes on UNIX and Linux will still run as processes (i.e. one Oracle process to one OS process), and other Oracle processes will run as threads within OS processes. For example, PMON and DBW might run as operating system processes, whereas LGWR and SMON might run as threads within a single process. The V$PROCESS view contains one row for each Oracle process connected to a database instance. This view can be queried to determine the operating system process ID and operating system thread ID for each process.

When running in multi-threaded mode, the database must be administered by an account that is authenticated through a password file. Attempting to start an instance that has been set to run in threaded execution mode with an account that has not been authenticated through a password file will result in an ORA-1031 error:

```
SQL> ALTER SYSTEM SET threaded_execution=true SCOPE=SPFILE;

System altered.

SQL> shutdown immediate
Database closed.
Database dismounted.
ORACLE instance shut down.
SQL> startup
ORA-01017: invalid username/password; logon denied
SQL>
```

## Use Flash Cache

The Database Smart Flash Cache allows an instance to access multiple flash devices without requiring a volume manager. The feature is supported only for databases running on the Solaris or Oracle Linux operating systems. Enabling the Smart Flash Cache may be beneficial if the following are true:

- The Buffer Pool Advisory section of your Automatic Workload Repository (AWR) report or STATSPACK report indicates that doubling the size of the buffer cache would be beneficial.
- db file sequential read is a top wait event.
- The system has spare CPU cycles.

There are two initialization parameters used to configure Database Smart Flash Cache:

- **DB_FLASH_CACHE_FILE** -- Specifies a list of paths and file names for the files to contain Database Smart Flash Cache. The files can be on the OS file system or an ASM disk group, but they must reside on a flash device. Configuring Database Smart Flash Cache on a disk drive (spindle) can negatively impact performance. If a specified file does not exist, then the database creates it during startup. A maximum of sixteen files is supported.
- **DB_FLASH_CACHE_SIZE** -- Specifies the size of each file in your Database Smart Flash Cache. Each size corresponds (in order) with a file specified in DB_FLASH_CACHE_FILE. If the number of sizes does not match the number of files, an error is generated. The size is expressed as nG, indicating the number of gigabytes (GB).

The V$FLASHFILESTAT view can be used to determine the cumulative latency and read counts of each file and compute the average latency. It is possible to disable a flash device by using the ALTER SYSTEM command to set the DB_FLASH_CACHE_SIZE to zero. Setting the size for any disabled flash device back to the original size will re-enable it. It is not possible to use ALTER SYSTEM to dynamically change the size of Database Smart Flash Cache.

# Index and Table Enhancements

## Use Index enhancements

It is now possible to create multiple indexes on the same set of columns in 12c. There must be a tangible difference between the two indexes (such as B-tree vs. bitmap) when the same columns are used. Also, when more than one index exists on the same set of columns, only one of them can be visible at a given time. The optimizer will never 'choose' between the multiple indexes on the same column set because it will never see more than one of them at the same time.

Multiple indexes can be created on the same set of columns when at least one of the following index characteristics is different:

- B-tree versus bitmap
- Different partitioning strategies
- Unique versus nonunique

## Use Table enhancements

It is now possible to control the visibility of table columns. When one or more columns of a table have been set to invisible, a generic access of the table will only display the visible columns. For example, the following operations will not display invisible columns:

- SELECT * FROM statements in SQL
- DESCRIBE commands in SQL*Plus
- %ROWTYPE attribute declarations in PL/SQL
- Describes in Oracle Call Interface (OCI)

Invisible columns will be displayed when explicitly referenced in a SELECT statement. Likewise, it is possible to insert a value into an invisible column by explicitly referencing it in the column list of an INSERT statement.

When an INSERT contains no column list, the statement can only insert values into visible columns.

Columns can be made invisible during table creation, when a column is added to a table, or by altering table to make a visible column invisible. Virtual columns can be invisible. You can use an invisible column as a partitioning key during table creation. Invisible columns have the following restrictions:

- External, cluster, and temporary tables cannot have invisible columns.
- Attributes of user-defined types cannot be invisible

## Use Online operation enhancements

Online table redefinition provides a means for making table structure modifications without significantly affecting the availability of the table. When a table is redefined online, it is accessible to both queries and DML during much of the redefinition process. The table is locked in the exclusive mode only during a very small portion of the total process. Online table redefinition can be performed with the Oracle EM Cloud Control Reorganize Objects wizard or with the DBMS_REDEFINITION package. There are three enhancements to Oracle's online redefinition capability in Oracle 12c:

- **Multiple Partitions** -- It is now possible to redefine multiple partitions in a single redefinition session. This feature reduces the completion time to redefine a partitioned table. When multiple partitions are redefined simultaneously, multiple interim tables are required during the table redefinition process. There must be sufficient free space and undo space to complete the table redefinition.
- **Tables With VPD Policies** -- It is now possible to redefine tables that have Virtual Private Database (VPD) policies. The copy_vpd_opt parameter in the START_REDEF_TABLE procedure

can be set to handle VPD policies during online redefinition. The parameter can be set to the following values:

o **DBMS_REDEFINITION.CONS_VPD_NONE** -- This is the default and indicates there are no VPD policies on the original table. If this value is used, and the original table has VPD policies, an error is raised.

o **DBMS_REDEFINITION.CONS_VPD_AUTO** -- This value will copy the VPD policies automatically from the original table to the new table during online redefinition.

o **DBMS_REDEFINITION.CONS_VPD_MANUAL** -- This value is used when the VPD policies must be manually copied from the original table to the new table during online redefinition. VPD policies must be copied manually when there are column mappings between the original table and the interim table or when you want to add or modify VPD policies during online redefinition.

- **Lock Timeout for FINISH_REDEF_TABLE** -- It is now possible to specify a lock timeout in number of seconds during which time FINISH_REDEF_TABLE attempts to acquire an exclusive lock for swapping the source and interim tables. If the timeout expires, the operation will exit. Previously, the user had to wait indefinitely or force an exit of the online redefinition session.

- **REDEF_TABLE** -- This is a new procedure in the DBMS_REDEFINITION package. Normally online redefinition is a multi-step process. REDEF_TABLE is capable of performing online redefinition of a table's storage properties in a single step when changing the following properties:

o Tablespace changes, including a tablespace change for a table, partition, index, or LOB columns

o Compression type changes, including a compression type change for a table, partition, index key, or LOB columns

o For LOB columns, a change to SECUREFILE or BASICFILE storage

# ADR and Network Enhancements

## Explain ADR enhancements

The new data definition language log file in Oracle 12c has the same format and basic behavior as the alert log. If the ENABLE_DDL_LOGGING initialization parameter is set to TRUE, DDL statements issued in the database will be written out to the log. When this parameter is set to FALSE, DDL statements are not included in any log. The file will contains one log record for each DDL statement. Two files are generated with the same information, one in XML format and the other as plain text. The DDL log is stored in the log/ddl subdirectory of the ADR home and will be included in IPS incident packages. When ENABLE_DDL_LOGGING is set to true, the following DDL statements are written to the alert log:

- ALTER/CREATE/DROP/TRUNCATE CLUSTER
- ALTER/CREATE/DROP FUNCTION
- ALTER/CREATE/DROP INDEX
- ALTER/CREATE/DROP OUTLINE
- ALTER/CREATE/DROP PACKAGE
- ALTER/CREATE/DROP PACKAGE BODY
- ALTER/CREATE/DROP PROCEDURE
- ALTER/CREATE/DROP PROFILE
- ALTER/CREATE/DROP SEQUENCE
- CREATE/DROP SYNONYM
- ALTER/CREATE/DROP/RENAME/TRUNCATE TABLE
- ALTER/CREATE/DROP TRIGGER
- ALTER/CREATE/DROP TYPE
- ALTER/CREATE/DROP TYPE BODY
- DROP USER
- ALTER/CREATE/DROP VIEW

**Debug Log**

The debug log is designed to record conditions in the database that are unusual, but do not inhibit normal operation of the detecting component. The warnings written to the debug log are not serious enough to warrant an incident or to be stored in the alert log. They are recorded in the debug file because they might be useful in diagnosing a future problem. The debug log has the same format and basic behavior as the alert log, but it only contains information about unusual conditions that might need to be corrected. Offloading this information to the debug log reduces the amount of information that must be written to the alert log and trace files and improves the visibility of debug information. The debug log is included in IPS incident packages and the contents are intended for Oracle Support.

# Oracle Data Pump, SQL*Loader, External Tables and Online Operations Enhancements

## Use Oracle Data Pump enhancements

When performing a full database export, Data Pump has a new full transportable export option. A full transportable export is performed when the TRANSPORTABLE=ALWAYS parameter is specified along with the FULL parameter. This functionality exports all objects and data required to create a complete copy of the database. Two data movement methods are performed by Data Pump depending on whether the tablespaces are transportable or not:

- **Non-transportable tablespaces** -- Tablespaces like SYSTEM and SYSAUX that cannot be transported have both their metadata and data unloaded into the dump file set, using direct path unload and external tables.
- **Transportable tablespaces** -- For transportable tablespaces, only metadata unloaded into the dump file set. The contents of the tablespaces are moved when you the data files are copied to the target database.


There are several restrictions for performing a full transportable export, including:

- The DATAPUMP_EXP_FULL_DATABASE privilege is required to perform this operation.
- The default tablespace of the user performing the export must not be set to one of the tablespaces being transported.
- If the database being exported contains either encrypted tablespaces or tables with encrypted columns, the ENCRYPTION_PASSWORD parameter must be supplied.
- If there are encrypted tablespaces in the source database, the source and target databases must be on platforms with the same endianness.

- If the source platform and the target platform are of different endianness, then you must convert the data being transported so that it is in the format of the target platform.
- A full transportable export is not restartable.
- All objects with storage that are selected for export must have all of their storage segments either entirely within administrative, non-transportable tablespaces (SYSTEM / SYSAUX) or entirely within user-defined, transportable tablespaces. Storage for a single object cannot straddle the two kinds of tablespaces.

The new functionality can be used to move a non-CDB into a pluggable database (PDB) or to move a PDB into another PDB. Full transportable operations can reduce both the export time and import times required for a full export. When this option is used, table data does not need to be unloaded and reloaded and index structures in user tablespaces do not need to be re-created. The full transportable feature is ideal for moving a database to a new computer system or upgrading to a new release of Oracle.

There are two enhancements to the way Data Pump works with compression.

- **Compression on import** -- A new option has been added to impdp and to the DBMS_DATAPUMP package that allows the compression options for a table to be changed during the import operation. The TRANSFORM parameter of impdp has a new TABLE_COMPRESSION_CLAUSE. If NONE is specified, the table gets the default compression for the tablespace. When the value is a valid table compression clause (for example, NOCOMPRESS), tables are created with the specified compression. Specifying this transform changes the type of compression for all tables in the job.
- **Compression on export** -- A new option has been added expdp and the DBMS_DATAPUMP package to control the degree of compression used when creating an Oracle Data Pump dump file. The COMPRESSION parameter can be used to compress the entire

operation, the data only, the metadata only, or perform no compression. By default, only the metadata is compressed. The new parameter allows the DBA more control over the resources used during an export operation.

Other enhancements to Data Pump include:

- **Export View As a Table** -- A new expdp command-line option will cause Data Pump to export a view as a table. Rather than exporting the view definition, Data Pump will export a table definition and unload data from the view as if it were a table. When the dump file is imported, impdp will create a table using the table definition and insert the data
- **LOGTIME** -- The new LOGTIME command-line parameter will cause messages displayed during export and import operations be timestamped. The option is available in impdp, expdp, and the DBMS_DATAPUMP.SET_PARAMETER procedure. The valid values are:
  - **NONE** -- No timestamps on status or log file messages (the default)
  - **STATUS** -- timestamps on status messages only
  - **LOGTIME** -- timestamps on log file messages only
  - **ALL** -- timestamps on both status and log file messages
- **Audit Commands** -- Oracle Data Pump commands can now be audited.
- **No Logging Option** -- A new DISABLE_ARCHIVE_LOGGING option has been added to the TRANSFORM parameter of impdp and the DBMS_DATAPUMP package. When utilized, it will disable redo logging when loading data into tables and when creating indexes. When the option is used, the disk space required for redo logs during an Oracle Data Pump import will be smaller. After performing the import operation, the DBA should perform an RMAN backup. Other operations still generate redo, including CREATE and ALTER statements (except CREATE INDEX) and operations against the master table used by Oracle Data Pump.
- **Security** -- The ENCRYPTION_PWD_PROMPT parameter has been added to the expdp and impdp command line. The parameter is used to indicate whether the Oracle Data Pump client should

prompt for passwords or whether it should retrieve the value from the command line.

- **SecureFiles LOB as Default** – A new option for impdp and the DBMS_DATAPUMP package forces Oracle Data Pump to create all LOBs as SecureFiles LOBs. By default, Data Pump re-creates tables exactly as they existed in the exported database, so if a LOB column was a BasicFile LOB in the exported database, Data Pump attempts to re-create it as a BasicFile LOB in the imported database.

## Use SQL*Loader and External table enhancements

The new SQL*Loader express mode makes it possible to load data from a flat file by specifying only a table name. For the functionality to succeed, the file must contain only delimited data and the table columns must be all character, number, or datetime types. When running in express mode, no control file is used. SQL*Loader uses the table column definitions to determine the input field order and data types in the file. For other settings, it makes use of default values unless overridden with command-line parameters. The following example performs a basic load into the EMPLOYEES table:

```
sqlldr username TABLE=employees
```

By default, SQL*Loader express mode assumes the following values unless specified otherwise:

- **Data file** -- When none is specified, SQL*Loader looks for a file named [table_name].dat in the current directory.
- **Load method** -- By default external tables is used. For some errors, SQL*Loader express mode will automatically switched to direct path load.
- **Fields** -- The fields use the names, column types, and order from the destination table. Records are delimited by a comma, separated by a newline, have no enclosure and use left-right trimming.

- **DOP** -- The DEGREE_OF_PARALLELISM parameter is set to AUTO.
- **Date Format** -- The NLS settings are used.
- **Character Set** -- The NLS settings are used.
- **Append mode** -- New data is to be appended to the table if it already has data in it.
- **File Names** -- When a data file is not specified, the data, log, and bad files take the following default names. (The %p is replaced with the process ID of the Oracle Database slave process.):
  - **Data File** -- table-name.dat
  - **SQL*Loader Log File** -- table-name.log
  - **Oracle Database Log Files** -- table-name_%p.log_xt
  - **Bad File** -- table-name_%p.bad

The external table option of SQL*Loader makes use of directory objects to indicate where all data files are stored and where output files are created. The user performing this action must have READ access to the directory objects containing the data files, and WRITE access to the directory objects where the output files are created. If directory objects do not already exist for the location of a data file or output file, then SQL*Loader will generate the SQL statement to create one. If this is the case, the user executing the load must have the CREATE ANY DIRECTORY privilege. If the directory object(s) should be deleted at the end of the load, the user must also have the DROP ANY DIRECTORY privilege.

**Direct NFS**

The Oracle Direct NFS (dNFS) is an internal I/O layer that provides faster access to large NFS files than traditional NFS clients. By default in 12c, SQL*Loader and external tables will automatically use the new package for large files. The DNFS_ENABLE command-line parameter for SQL*Loader and access parameter for external tables can be used to explicitly control the use of dNFS. The Direct NFS Client interface is used by default when it reads data files over 1 GB. For smaller files, the operating system's I/O interfaces are used. To use the Direct NFS Client on all input data files, use DNFS_ENABLE=TRUE. To disable use of the Direct NFS Client for all data files, specify DNFS_ENABLE=FALSE.

# Partitioning Enhancements

## Explain Partitioning enhancements
### Interval-Reference Partitioning

In 12c reference-partitioned tables can use interval partitioning as a top partitioning strategy. Using interval partitioned tables as the parent for a reference partitioned table results in better partitioning modeling. Partitions in the reference partitioned table corresponding to interval partitions in the parent table are created upon insert into the reference partitioned table. Any operations that transform interval partitions to conventional partitions in the parent table will construct the corresponding transformation in the child table, creating partitions in the child table as necessary. Interval-reference functionality requires that the COMPATIBLE initialization parameter be set to greater than or equal to 12.0.0.0.

### Cascade Functionality

TRUNCATE PARTITION and EXCHANGE PARTITION operations for reference and interval-reference partitioned tables are able to cascade to reference partitioned child tables. This allows partition maintenance operation to be inherited from the parent to the child tables. By default cascade options are disabled so that they do not affect compatibility.

Exchange operations can be cascaded to reference partitioned child tables with the CASCADE option of the ALTER TABLE EXCHANGE PARTITION and ALTER TABLE EXCHANGE SUBPARTITION SQL statements. All foreign key constraints must be defined as ON DELETE CASCADE for cascading exchange operations to take place.

When the CASCADE option is specified, the EXCHANGE operation cascades to reference partitioned tables that are children of the targeted table. The CASCADE option is ignored if it is specified for a table that does not have reference partitioned children.

Similarly, the TRUNCATE TABLE, ALTER TABLE TRUNCATE PARTITION, and ALTER TABLE TRUNCATE SUBPARTITION SQL statements can cascade to reference partitioned tables through an enabled referential constraint that is set to ON DELETE CASCADE. The cascading action applies recursively to grandchildren, great-grandchildren, and so on. After determining the set of tables to be truncated based on the referential constraints, an error is raised if any table in the set is referenced through an enabled constraint from a child outside of the set. If a parent and child are connected by multiple referential constraints, a TRUNCATE TABLE CASCADE operation targeting the parent succeeds if at least one constraint has ON DELETE CASCADE enabled. When the CASCADE option is specified, the TRUNCATE PARTITION and TRUNCATE SUBPARTITION operations cascade to reference partitioned tables that are children of the targeted table.

## Maintenance Operations on Multiple Partitions

A number of partition maintenance operations can now be performed on multiple partitions with a single statement. This simplifies application development results in more efficient partition maintenance. The affected operations are:

- **ADD** -- Multiple new partitions and subpartitions can be added with the ADD PARTITION and ADD SUBPARTITION clauses of the ALTER TABLE statement. this capability is only supported for range, list, and system partitions and subpartitions. Multiple range partitions can be added to a range-partitioned or composite range-partitioned table, if that table does not have a MAXVALUE partition defined. Likewise, you can add multiple list partitions to a table using new sets of partition values if the table does not have a DEFAULT partition. The following example adds multiple partitions to the range-partitioned orders table:

```
ALTER TABLE orders ADD
PARTITION orders_2013 VALUES LESS THAN
     (TO_DATE('01-APR-2014','DD-MON-YYYY')),
PARTITION orders_2014 VALUES LESS THAN
     (TO_DATE('01-JUL-2015','DD-MON-YYYY')),
PARTITION orders_2015 VALUES LESS THAN
     (TO_DATE('01-JAN-2016','DD-MON-YYYY'));
```

- **DROP** -- It is possible to drop multiple partitions or subpartitions from a range or list partitioned table with the DROP PARTITION and DROP SUBPARTITION clauses of the SQL ALTER TABLE statement. It is not possible to drop all partitions of a table. The following SQL statement drops multiple partitions from the range-partitioned table orders:

```
ALTER TABLE orders DROP PARTITION
   orders_1999, orders_2000,
   orders_2001, orders_2002;
```

- **TRUNCATE** -- It is possible to truncate multiple partitions from a range or list partitioned table with the TRUNCATE PARTITION clause of the ALTER TABLE statement. Global indexes must be rebuilt unless UPDATE INDEXES is specified. The following example truncates multiple partitions in the range-partitioned orders table:

```
ALTER TABLE sales TRUNCATE PARTITIONS
   orders_1999, orders_2000,
   orders_2001, orders_2002;
```

- **MERGE** -- The ALTER TABLE MERGE PARTITION statement can be used to merge the contents of two or more partitions into one. The two original partitions are dropped, as are any corresponding local indexes. This statement cannot be used for a hash partitioned table or for hash subpartitions. When merging multiple range partitions, the partitions must be adjacent and specified in the ascending order of their partition bound values. The following example merges four partitions in the orders table into one partition:

```
ALTER TABLE orders
MERGE PARTITIONS orders_2003, orders_2004,
                 orders_2005, orders_2006
INTO PARTITION orders_2003_6;
```

Alternately, the statement could have been written:

```
ALTER TABLE orders
MERGE PARTITIONS orders_2003 TO orders_2006
INTO PARTITION orders_2003_6;
```

- **SPLIT** -- The contents of one partition or subpartition can be split into multiple partitions or subpartitions with the SPLIT PARTITION and SPLIT SUBPARTITION clauses of the ALTER TABLE statement. After a split operation, the original segment is discarded. The new partitions are in separate segments and inherit all unspecified physical attributes from the source partition. The following example splits the orders partitions that were merged above:

```
ALTER TABLE orders
SPLIT PARTITION orders_2003_6 INTO
( PARTITION orders_2003 VALUES LESS THAN
      (TO_DATE('01-JAN-2004','DD-MON-YYYY')),
  PARTITION orders_2004 VALUES LESS THAN
      (TO_DATE('01-JAN-2005','DD-MON-YYYY')),
  PARTITION orders_2005 VALUES LESS THAN
      (TO_DATE('01-JAN-2006','DD-MON-YYYY')),
  PARTITION orders_2006 VALUES LESS THAN
      (TO_DATE('01-JAN-2007','DD-MON-YYYY'))
);
```

**Online Move Partition**

This feature allows partitions to be moved or redefined while DML operations continue to run uninterrupted on the partition that altered. Global indexes for the table continue to be maintained during the move partition, so a manual index rebuild is not required. The MOVE PARTITION clause of the ALTER TABLE statement can be used to perform the following tasks:

- Re-cluster data and reduce fragmentation
- Move a partition to another tablespace
- Modify create-time attributes
- Store the data in compressed format using table compression

It is possible to alter many of the physical storage attributes of a partition using an ALTER TABLE/INDEX MODIFY PARTITION statement. For physical attributes that cannot be changed using that method (such as TABLESPACE) you should use the MOVE PARTITION clause. In addition, while it is possible to use MODIFY PARTITION to change the compression, the statement affects only future storage, but not existing data. Using the MOVE PARTITION clause, it is possible to alter the compression of existing and future data. When the MOVE PARTITION clause is used, the old segment is always dropped and a new segment created, even it is being recreated in the same tablespace. For an interval or interval-* partitioned table, it is only possible to move range partitions or interval partitions that have been materialized. A partition in a reference-partitioned table can be moved independently of the partition in the master table.

# Explain Index enhancements for partitioned tables
## Asynchronous Global Index Maintenance

The partition maintenance operations DROP PARTITION and TRUNCATE PARTITION have been optimized in 12c by making the index maintenance for metadata only. By default, the maintenance on global indexes for these operations is asynchronous. These operations can now be performed without rendering a global index unusable. The global index maintenance after the DROP or TRUNCATE operation can be performed during off-peak hours without impacting the index availability. This makes partition and subpartition maintenance operations faster and less resource intensive at the time of the operation. The UPDATE INDEXES clause is still required in order to provide backward compatibility. There are several limitations of asynchronous global index maintenance:

- Only applicable for heap tables
- Tables with object types are not supported
- Tables with domain indexes are not supported
- Not performed for the user SYS

The automatic scheduler job SYS.PMO_DEFERRED_GIDX_MAINT_JOB can be used to clean up all global indexes requiring maintenance. By default, this job is scheduled to run at 2:00 A.M. on a daily basis. It can be run at any time using DBMS_SCHEDULER.RUN_JOB to proactively clean up the indexes.

**Partial Indexes**

For partitioned tables, it is now possible to create local and global indexes on a subset of the partitions. This allows greater flexibility in index creation for partitioned tables. When a table is created or altered, a default indexing property can be specified for the table or its partitions. This property is only considered for partial indexes. Partial indexing is not supported for unique indexes, or for indexes used to enforce unique constraints. By default, any index is created as a FULL index, which decouples the index from the table indexing property. The INDEXING clause may also be specified at the partition and subpartition levels. The following example creates the partitioned table SALES:

```
CREATE TABLE sales (
sls_id        NUMBER,
cst_id        NUMBER,
sale_date     DATE,
sale_total    NUMBER(9,2))
INDEXING OFF
PARTITION BY RANGE (SALE_DATE)
(PARTITION sls_p1 VALUES LESS THAN
     (TO_DATE('01-JAN-11','DD-MON-YY'))
 INDEXING OFF,
 PARTITION sla_p2 VALUES LESS THAN
     (TO_DATE('01-JAN-12','DD-MON-YY'))
 INDEXING ON,
 PARTITION sla_p3 VALUES LESS THAN
     (TO_DATE('01-JAN-13','DD-MON-YY'))
 INDEXING ON,
 PARTITION sls_p4 VALUES LESS THAN
     (TO_DATE('01-JAN-14','DD-MON-YYY'))
 INDEXING ON,
 PARTITION sls_p5 VALUES LESS THAN
     (TO_DATE('01-JAN-15','DD-MON-YY'))
);
```

The partial indexing behavior for the above statement is:

- Partitions SLS_P2, SLS_P3, and SLS_P4 are included in all partial global indexes
- Local index partitions (for indexes created PARTIAL) corresponding to the above three table partitions are created usable by default.
- Other partitions are excluded from all partial global indexes, and created unusable in local indexes (for indexes created PARTIAL).

## ONLINE Move Partition

The ALTER TABLE ... MOVE PARTITION operation now allows DML operations continue to run uninterrupted on the partition that is being moved. During the move partition, global indexes are maintained, so a manual index rebuild is no longer required.

# SQL Enhancements

## Use Oracle Database Migration Assistant for Unicode

The Database Migration Assistant for Unicode (DMU) ships with Oracle Database 12c Release 1 (12.1) and is now the officially supported method for migration to the Unicode character set. The legacy Database Character Set Scanner (CSSCAN) and CSALTER utilities have been removed from the database installation and are de-supported.

DMU guides the DBA through the entire migration process and automates many of the migration tasks. For post-migration and existing databases already using the Unicode character set, the DMU has a validation mode. The validation mode identifies data not correctly encoded in Unicode to identify potential issues with implementation of Unicode in database applications.

A database must meet certain requirements to be supported by the DMU, including:

- The release of Oracle Database must be 10.2.0.4, 10.2.0.5, 11.1.0.7, 11.2.0.1, or later.
- The database character set must be ASCII-based.
- The SYS.DBMS_DUMA_INTERNAL package must be installed in the database.
- Oracle Database Vault must be disabled before starting the migration process.
- The database cannot be a 12c Pluggable Database (PDB).
- The database must be opened in read/write mode.

Some of the features of the DMU include:

- **Selective Conversion** -- The DMU has the ability to process only the data that must be converted, at the table, column, and row level.
- **Monitoring** -- DMU includes a GUI to visualize the conversion progress.

- **Inline Conversion** -- Oracle Database supports inline conversion of database contents using the DMU.
- **Scheduling** -- Cleansing actions can be scheduled for later execution during the conversion step.

Before it is possible to convert a database to Unicode, DMU must analyze the character data in VARCHAR2, CHAR, LONG, and CLOB table columns. This process will determine if any issues exist that would cause the conversion to corrupt data. The DMU converts character column values in the database from their declared character set to the target Unicode character set. It then checks each value for the following problems:

- The conversion result differs from the original value.
- The conversion result fits into the length limit of its column.
- The conversion result fits into its data type.
- The conversion result does not contain any replacement characters, that is, each converted source character code is valid in the declared character set of the column.

## Use Row limiting clause, and secure file LOBs enhancements

Until now, there has been no simple means for creating top-N SQL queries in Oracle. Queries that limited the number of rows returned by a query using the ROWNUM psuedo column returned data before the ORDER BY operation occurred, and so did not produce the 'Top-N' results. Two new clauses, FETCH FIRST and OFFSET provide native SQL language support for this capability. It is now possible with a simple SQL statement to limit the number of rows returned and to specify a starting row for the return set. The following queries demonstrate how to use the clauses.

The following statement returns the four employees with the highest salary:

```
SELECT first_name, last_name, salary
FROM   hr.employees
ORDER BY salary DESC
FETCH FIRST 4 ROWS ONLY;
```

```
FIRST_NAME    LAST_NAME      SALARY
-----------   -----------   --------
Steven        King            24000
Neena         Kochhar         17000
Lex           De Haan         17000
John          Russell         14000
```

Note that there is no such thing as a "FETCH LAST" command. To return the highest N numbers, you must sort the data in descending order. The next example skips the highest four rows and returns the employees with next five highest salaries:

```
SELECT first_name, last_name, salary
FROM   hr.employees
ORDER BY salary DESC
OFFSET 4 ROWS FETCH NEXT 5 ROWS ONLY;
```

```
FIRST_NAME    LAST_NAME      SALARY
-----------   -----------   --------
Karen         Partners        13500
Michael       Hartstein       13000
Nancy         Greenberg       12008
Shelley       Higgins         12008
Alberto       Errazuriz       12000
```

It is also possible to supply a percentage with the FETCH NEXT rather than a set number of rows. The following statement returns the 4 percent of employees with the highest salaries:

```
SELECT first_name, last_name, salary
FROM    hr.employees
ORDER BY salary DESC
FETCH NEXT 4 PERCENT ROWS ONLY;


FIRST_NAME    LAST_NAME      SALARY
------------  -----------  --------
Steven        King            24000
Neena         Kochhar         17000
Lex           De Haan         17000
John          Russell         14000
Karen         Partners        13500
```

## SecureFiles

With Oracle 12c, SecureFiles is now the default for LOB storage when the COMPATIBLE parameter is set to 12.1 or higher. SecureFiles feature provides improved performance over BasicFiles for storing unstructured data. The following enhancements have been made to SecureFiles in this release:

- **PDML Operations** -- SecureFiles have enhanced support for parallel DML operations. Non-partitioned tables that contain SecureFile LOB columns (and no BasicFile LOB columns) can support parallel DML. Operations that can be parallelized include:
  - INSERT
  - INSERT AS SELECT
  - CREATE TABLE AS SELECT
  - DELETE
  - UPDATE
  - MERGE (conditional UPDATE and INSERT)
  - Multi-table INSERT
  - SQL Loader
  - Import/Export
- **LogMiner** -- LogMiner now fully supports SecureFiles LOBs, including support for deduplication of SecureFiles LOB columns and SecureFiles Database File System (DBFS) operations when database compatibility is set to 11.2 or later. Only SQL_REDO columns can be filled in for SecureFiles LOB columns; SQL_UNDO columns are not filled in.

## Configure extended data types

The maximum size of VARCHAR2, NVARCHAR2, and RAW data types in Oracle 12c has been increased to 32767 bytes. The initialization parameter MAX_STRING_SIZE determines whether or not a given database supports the extended limits. If the value is set to STANDARD (the default), the pre-12c limits apply: 4000 bytes for VARCHAR2 and NVARCHAR2 and 2000 bytes for RAW. When the parameter is set to EXTENDED, the data types can use the full 32767 bytes.

When a VARCHAR2 or NVARCHAR2 column is declared with more than 4000 bytes, or a RAW data type with more than 2000 bytes, they are considered an extended data type. Extended data type columns use Oracle's LOB technology to store the data out-of-line. In tablespaces managed with Automatic Segment Space Management (ASSM), extended data type columns are stored as SecureFiles LOBs. Otherwise, they are stored as BasicFile LOBs. The storage mechanism is handled internally by the database. The columns do not appear as LOBs in user-visible operations and the columns cannot be manipulated using the DBMS_LOB package.

# Key DBA Skills

## Core Administration

### Explain the fundamentals of DB architecture

The Oracle Relational Database Management System (RDBMS) is an immensely capable (and complex) application designed to provide a comprehensive, open, and integrated information management system. It can manage huge amounts of data in a multiuser environment to provide concurrent access to data for thousands of simultaneous users. It provides a high level of data security, excellent performance, and has extremely effective failure recovery capabilities.

**Database vs. Instance**

At the highest level, an Oracle database server consists of two distinct components: a database and one or more database instances. In general usage, the term Oracle database is often used to refer to both. The definitions of the two are:

- **Database** – A database is a set of files, located on disk, that store data. These files can exist independently of a database instance.
- **Database instance** – An instance is a set of memory structures that manage database files. An Oracle instance consists of a shared memory area and a set of background processes. An instance can exist independently of database files.

In the conventional configuration, there is a single instance and a single database. However, when using Real Application Clusters, there are multiple instances pointing at a single database. The RAC configuration allows for improved scalability, performance, and fault tolerance.

Oracle Data Guard is a configuration where a primary database server is related to one or more standby databases. Standby databases may be physical standbys that are byte-for-byte copies of the primary and are kept current through the application of redo logs from the primary. Alternately they can be logical standbys which are kept synchronized by SQL statements propagated through Oracle Streams.

The illustration below shows the primary components of an Oracle instance. There is a view on the Oracle Learning Library that breaks the instance components out to a much more granular level and also shows the database elements as well:

(http://www.oracle.com/webfolder/technetwork/tutorials/obe/db/12c/r 1/poster/OUTPUT_poster/poster.html). You do not have to memorize either diagram, but they help you to visualize how the various aspects of the Oracle instance fit together.

Figure 1: Oracle instance components

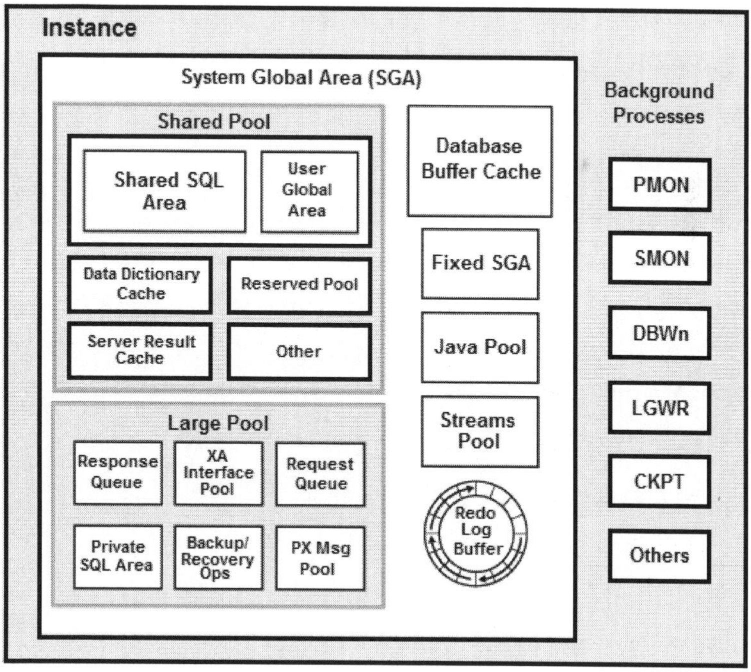

When an Oracle instance is started, background processes are initiated and a memory area is allocated in the operating system. This memory area stores numerous different pieces of information required to run the database. Some of the basic memory structures are:

- **System Global Area (SGA)** – The SGA is a group of shared memory structures that contain data and control information for a single Oracle Database instance. The SGA is shared by all server and background processes. Examples of data stored in the SGA include cached data blocks and shared SQL areas.
- **Program global area (PGA)** – A PGA is a memory region that is not shared. It contains data and control information exclusively for the use of an Oracle process. A PGA is created when an Oracle process is started. One PGA exists for each server process and background process. The collection of individual PGAs is the total instance PGA, or instance PGA.
- **User Global Area (UGA)** – The UGA is memory associated with a user session.
- **Software code areas** – Software code areas are portions of memory used to store code that is being run or can be run.

**System Global Area**

The SGA is the memory container for all of the data required for the database instance. It consists of numerous memory components. Each component is a pool of memory used to satisfy a particular type of memory allocation request. All except the redo log buffer allocate and deallocate space in units of contiguous memory called granules. You can query the V$SGASTAT view for information about SGA components.

The most important elements of the SGA are:

- **Database Buffer Cache** – The database buffer cache stores copies of data blocks read from data files. A buffer is an address where the buffer manager temporarily caches a currently or recently used data block. All users connected to a database instance share access to the buffer cache. The buffer cache is designed to optimize physical I/O; to keep frequently accessed blocks in the buffer cache; and to write infrequently accessed blocks to disk. It makes use of a Least Recently Used (LRU) algorithm to determine what information should be kept in the buffer cache.

- **Redo Log Buffer** – The redo log buffer is a circular buffer that stores redo entries describing changes made to the database. These entries contain the information required to reconstruct changes made to the database by DML or DDL operations. Database recovery applies redo entries to data files to reconstruct lost changes. The redo entries take up continuous, sequential space in the buffer. The background process log writer (LGWR) writes the redo log buffer to the active online redo log group on disk.
- **Shared Pool** – The shared pool caches various types of program data required by the server. A partial list includes storing parsed SQL, PL/SQL code, system parameters, and data dictionary information. It is involved in almost every operation that occurs in the database. Among other things, every SQL statement issued by users requires an access of the shared pool.
- **Large Pool** – The large pool is an optional memory area in the SGA. It is intended for memory allocations that are larger than is appropriate to store in the shared pool. Examples of this are the UGA for the shared server and the Oracle XA interface and buffers for Recovery Manager (RMAN) I/O slaves.
- **Java Pool** – The Java pool stores all session-specific Java code and data within the Java Virtual Machine (JVM). This includes Java objects that are migrated to the Java session space at end-of-call.
- **Streams Pool** – The Streams pool is used exclusively by Oracle Streams. It stores buffered queue messages and provides memory for Streams capture and apply processes. Unless configured otherwise, the size of the Streams pool starts at zero and grows dynamically as required by Oracle Streams.
- **Fixed SGA** – The fixed SGA is an internal housekeeping area. Among other things, it contains general information required by the background processes about the state of the database and the instance. The size of the fixed SGA is set by the Oracle Database and cannot be altered manually.

## Install and configure a database

The earlier topic in the 'New Features' section: "Use OUI, DBCA for installation and configuration" covered this information. I considered splitting the information into two pieces or covering it twice, but that made no sense.

## Configure server and client network for a database

Oracle Net Services is the element that provides connectivity solutions in distributed computing environments. One component of Oracle Net Services, Oracle Net, enables a network session from a client application to an Oracle Database server. Any time a network session is established between a client application and the database, Oracle Net acts as the data courier. It establishes and maintains the connection between the client application and the database. Throughout the life of the session it is integral in exchanging messages between them. Oracle Net enables connections from traditional client/server applications to Oracle Database servers. Oracle Net resides on both the client and the database server and communicates with TCP/IP to facilitate connectivity and data transfer between the client and the database. The graphic below shows how Oracle Net enables a network connection between a client and a database server. There are several other connection types possible: Java Application connections, Web Client connections through Application Web Server, and others. See the Oracle Database Net Services Administrator's Guide for more details.

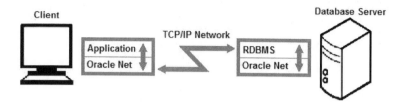

Figure 3: Oracle Net client-server connection

On the client computer, Oracle Net is a background component that facilitates application connections to the database. On the server side, the Oracle Net Listener coordinates connections between the database and client connections. While the most common use of Oracle Net Services is to handle incoming Oracle database connections, it can also be used as an interface to non Oracle data sources (such as SQL Server and DB2) or to access external code libraries via EXTPROC.

The Oracle Database server receives the initial connection through Oracle Net Listener (referred to henceforth as the listener). The listener is an Oracle background process that listens on a specific port for database connection requests. It brokers a client request and hands off the request to the server. The listener is configured with a protocol address. Clients configured to use that protocol address can send connection requests to the listener. Once a connection has been established, the client and Oracle server communicate directly with one another. Stopping the listener will prevent new connections from occurring, but will not affect existing connections.

In order to connect to a database service, clients must use a connect descriptor that provides both the location of the database and the name of the database service. The following example is an Easy Connect descriptor that connects to a database service named ocp.exam.com, and the host ocp-server (by default the port that will be used is 1521):  ocp-server/ocp.exam.com

In order for the above connection to work, the database being connected to must have a matching entry in the configuration file tnsnames.ora. The matching entry in that file for the preceding connect descriptor and database service would be:

```
(DESCRIPTION=
(ADDRESS=(PROTOCOL=tcp)(HOST=ocp-server)(PORT=1521))
(CONNECT_DATA=
(SERVICE_NAME=ocp.exam.com)))
```

A connect descriptor is a specially formatted description of the destination for a network connection. It contains the destination service and network route information. The destination service is indicated by name and the network route by the location of the listener through the use of a network address. A connect descriptor is comprised of one or more protocol addresses of the listener and the connect information for the destination service in the tnsnames.ora file. The below example is a connect descriptor for the ocp database.

```
ocp=
(DESCRIPTION=
      (ADDRESS=(PROTOCOL=tcp)
               (HOST=ocp-server)
               (PORT=1521)
      )
      (CONNECT_DATA=(SID=ocp)
                    (SERVICE_NAME=ocp.exam.com)
                    (INSTANCE_NAME=ocp)
      )
)
```

The ADDRESS section contains the following parameters:

- **PROTOCOL** – Identifies the listener protocol address. The protocol 'tcp' is used for TCP/IP.
- **HOST** – Identifies the host name. The host is ocp-server. You can also use an IP address when using the TCP/IP protocol.
- **PORT** – Identifies the port. 1521 is the default port used by Oracle Net.

The CONNECT_DATA section contains the following parameters:

- **SID** – Identifies the SID of the Oracle database. In this case the SID is ocp.
- **SERVICE_NAME** – Identifies the service. The destination service name is a database service named ocp.exam.com. The value for this parameter comes from the SERVICE_NAMES initialization parameter. Generally the SERVICE_NAMES parameter is the global database name.
- **INSTANCE_NAME** – Identifies the database instance. This parameter is optional and defaults to the SID entered during installation or database creation.

When the database is in a dedicated server configuration, the listener starts a separate dedicated server process for each incoming client connection. The server process thus created is dedicated to servicing the one client. When the session is complete, the dedicated server process terminates. The steps for the listener passing a client connection request to a dedicated server process and the establishment of a database session follow:

1. The listener receives a client connection request.
2. The listener starts a dedicated server process, and the dedicated server inherits the connection request from the listener.
3. The client is now connected directly to the dedicated server.
4. The server process checks the client's authentication credentials.
5. If credentials are valid, a session to the database is created.

When connecting to the Oracle database from a client computer, there must be some method for the client computer to know where the Oracle server is on the network and what port it is listening on. Configuring the client network is the act of determining the means by which clients are able to resolve the address of the Oracle server when connecting to it. There are several methods that can be used to provide this information:

## Local Naming Method

The local naming method uses the TNSNAMES.ORA file to provide the client with the required address. By default, this file is located in the ORACLE_HOME/network/admin directory. Network service names and connect descriptors are stored in the file. The following example shows a network service name sales mapped to a connect descriptor.

```
ocprep=
(DESCRIPTION=
    (ADDRESS=(PROTOCOL=tcp)(HOST=ocprep-server)(PORT=1521))
    (CONNECT_DATA=
    (SERVICE_NAME=ocprep.us.example.com)))
```

The DESCRIPTION section of a connect description identifies the destination database service and determines the protocol to be used when making the connection. The above example uses TCP/IP as the protocol on port 1521. It is possible to configure local naming during installation or afterward. During the installation, the Oracle Net Configuration Assistant prompts you to configure network service names. After installation, you can configure the local naming method via Oracle Net Configuration Assistant, Oracle Enterprise Manager Cloud Control, or Oracle Net Manager

## Easy Connect Naming Method

The Easy Connect naming method bypasses performing a service name lookup in the TNSNAMES.ORA file. When using Easy Connect no naming or directory system is required at all. It enables clients to connect to a database server using the host name of the database and an optional port and service name. The basic format is:

```
CONNECT
username@[//]host[:port][/service_name][:server][/instance_name]
```

The connect identifier used by EZ Connect corresponds to the following TNSNAMES.ORA connect descriptor:

```
(DESCRIPTION=
    (ADDRESS=(PROTOCOL=tcp)(HOST=host)(PORT=port))
    (CONNECT_DATA=
    (SERVICE_NAME=service_name)
    (SERVER=server)
    (INSTANCE_NAME=instance_name)))
```

The default service name when Oracle is installed in Typical mode is the database name. The Easy Connect syntax used to connect to that instance would be:

```
SQLPLUS /nolog
SQL> CONNECT username@host/db_name
SQL> Enter password: password
```

Using the connect descriptor example from the Local Naming Method above, the full Easy Connect syntax would be:

```
CONNECT username@ocprep-server:1521/ocprep.us.example.com
```

Clients can use Easy Connect naming if all of the following conditions are met:

- Oracle Net Services software is installed on the client.
- Oracle TCP/IP protocol is supported on both the client and database server.
- No features, such as external procedure calls, or Heterogeneous Services, require a more advanced connect descriptor.
- EZCONNECT is specified by the NAMES.DIRECTORY_PATH parameter in the sqlnet.ora file.

## Directory Naming Method

The directory naming method makes use of an LDAP-compliant directory server such as Oracle Internet Directory. When using this method, connect identifiers are mapped to connect descriptors in the directory server. An LDAP directory provides centralized administration of database services and network service names.

A database service entry is created during the installation of the Oracle database. Once the installation is completed, it is possible to use Oracle Enterprise Manager Cloud Control or Oracle Net Manager to configure clients to use the directory naming method. With them you can create or modify network service names and network service alias entries, and to modify the database service entry. Once configured, clients can use the directory entries to connect to the database.

## External Naming Methods

External naming makes use of a third-party naming service such as network information services (NIS). This allows clients to resolve network service names to a network address. Companies that are making use of NIS can make use of it to store network service names and addresses with NIS external naming. When a client program attempts to connect to a database using a network service name, the NIS server will resolve it to an Oracle Net address and return the address to the client. The client program then uses this address to connect to Oracle Database.

# Monitor database alerts

The background processes and servers that make up an Oracle instance each have their own trace file. If a process detects an error condition, it will dump information about the error out to its particular trace file. Some of the trace file information is intended for the use of the database administrator, and the remainder is for Oracle Support. In addition to the trace files, there is the database alert log. It contains a chronological list of messages and errors from the database. Some of the messages recorded in the alert log include:

- Initialization parameters with non-default values at instance startup.
- All occurrences of the following errors: internal (ORA-600), block corruption (ORA-1578), and deadlock (ORA-60).
- Many administrative commands, including CREATE, ALTER, and DROP DDL statements as well as STARTUP and SHUTDOWN.

The alert log is maintained simultaneously in two versions: an XML-formatted file and a text-formatted file. Either version of the alert log can be viewed with a text editor. Alternately, the ADRCI utility can be used to view the XML-formatted version with the XML tags removed. One of the duties of a DBA is to periodically check the alert log and trace files to see if the server or any background processes have encountered errors. The alert log and trace files are written out to directories that are part of the Automatic Diagnostic Repository. Trace file names generally include the name of the process that writes to the file, such as MMON and LGWR. The MAX_DUMP_FILE_SIZE can be used to limit the file size of trace files to the specified number of operating system blocks. It is not possible to limit the size of the alert log. You must periodically delete the file to control the size. This can be done while the instance is running. Generally, you should create an archive copy prior to deleting the file.

Any time a critical error occurs, one or more trace files will be written on behalf of the involved server processes. In addition, if the SQL_TRACE initialization parameter is set to TRUE, the SQL trace facility will generate performance statistics for all SQL statements processed by the instance. These traces are then written to the ADR. Alternately, SQL tracing can be enabled at a session level by issuing the command ALTER SESSION SET

SQL_TRACE. The DBMS_SESSION and DBMS_MONITOR packages can be used to control SQL tracing for a session.

### Adaptive Thresholds

It's possible to monitor database performance continuously using adaptive thresholds. The DBA can set warning and critical alert thresholds for numerous system metrics. These thresholds are created using statistics derived from metrics captured in the moving window baseline. The statistics for the moving window metrics are recomputed weekly and may result in new thresholds if the system performance changes. Adaptive thresholds can detect different workload patterns of the database, such as OLTP activity during the day, batch processing at night, and backups on the weekend. Once detected, it will automatically set different threshold values for the performance pattern detected.

There are two types of adaptive thresholds:

**Percentage of maximum** – The threshold value is computed as a percentage multiple of the maximum value observed for the data in the moving window baseline (for example 95% of the maximum value observed).

**Significance level** – The threshold value is set to a percentile representing how unusual it is to observe values above the threshold. It is set to one of the following percentiles:

- **High (.95)** – Only 5 in 100 observations are expected to exceed this value.
- **Very High (.99)** – Only 1 in 100 observations are expected to exceed this value.
- **Severe (.999)** – Only 1 in 1,000 observations are expected to exceed this value.
- **Extreme (.9999)** – Only 1 in 10,000 observations are expected to exceed this value.

# Perform daily administration tasks

The specific 'daily' administration tasks for an Oracle database vary significantly depending on the company, the database, and the database administrator. Two DBAs that have the same set of 'daily tasks' to perform may do them in very different ways. Some database administrators (including myself) like spending time on the front end to automate as much of the repetitive grunt-work as possible. Others prefer to stay hands-on with all of their tasks.

The Oracle Database Administrator's Guide provides the following list as the tasks of a DBA:

- Installing and upgrading the Oracle Database server and application tools
- Allocating system storage and planning future storage requirements for the database system
- Creating primary database storage structures (tablespaces)
- Creating primary objects (tables, views, indexes)
- Planning for backup and recovery of database information
- Contacting Oracle for technical support
- Ensuring compliance with Oracle license agreements
- Modifying the database structure, as necessary
- Enrolling users and maintaining system security
- Controlling and monitoring user access to the database
- Monitoring and optimizing the performance of the database
- Maintaining archived data on tape
- Backing up and restoring the database

I have ordered the list so that the duties performed least often are towards the top and the duties performed most often are towards the bottom. I would consider only the bottom four to be 'daily; tasks, but I could make a case for including the bottom six. Of the daily tasks, I would argue that the backup and recovery tasks are the most critical for an Oracle DBA. A production database not only needs to have a viable backup strategy, but DBAs must check to ensure that the strategy is occurring as intended. Automating the backup strategy and then ignoring it is a recipe for disaster.

Doctors take an oath to 'do no harm.' If there were an oath for database administrators, it would have to be 'lose no data.' Maintaining the database at peak performance is important. So is keeping the users in-line and happy. Ensuring that no data gets lost is <u>absolutely essential</u>.

## Apply and review patches

You can locate patches and their metadata files at the My Oracle support website. The steps to do this are:

- Log in to My Oracle Support (https://support.oracle.com/)
- Click the Patches & Updates tab
- On the Patches & Updates page, in the Patch Search section, enter the patch number you want to search for, and click Search.
- On the Patch Search Results page, click the patch number. My Oracle Support displays details of the patch in a collapsible frame.
- Click Download.
- In the File Download dialog, click the name of the patch zip file to download it to your local host.
- Click Download Patch Metadata.
- In the Download Patch Metadata dialog, click Download to download the patch metadata file.

After installation and on a regular basis, DBAs should download and install patches to the Oracle software. There are several varieties of patches produced by Oracle, including:

- **Interim Patches** -- These contain a single bug fix or a collection of bug fixes provided as required. They may also be one-offs for customer-specific security bug fixes.
- **Diagnostic Patches** -- These are intended to help diagnose or verify a fix or a collection of bug fixes.

- **Patch Set Updates (PSU)** -- These contain a collection of high impact, low risk, and proven fixes for a specific product or component.
- **Critical Patch Updates (CPU)** -- A collection of patches for multiple security vulnerabilities.

Some patches can be installed while the database is running using either OPatch or the Enterprise Manager Patch Wizard (which uses opatch in the background). You can determine what patches are applicable to your system through the Patch Advisor in Enterprise Manager Cloud Control.

**Online Patches**

Prior to release 11g of Oracle, all patches contained .o (object) files and/or .a (archive) libraries. Installing them required a relink of the RDBMS binary and therefore meant the database had to be shut down before the patch could be applied. Now an increasingly large number of patches are available as online patches. These contain .so files, which are dynamic/shared libraries, and they do not require a relink of the RDBMS binary. Because a relink is not needed, online patches can be applied or rolled back while the database instance is running. This simplifies administration, because no downtime is needed. It also means that installing or de-installing Online Patches is faster – potentially taking just a few seconds. Online patches will be installed using the opatch utility.

The benefits of online patches include the following:

- No downtime is required
- They persist across shutdowns
- They allow rolling patches in RAC
- They have a fast installation

There are few downsides to online patches:

- They require more memory
- Online patching isn't available on all platforms
- Not all patches are available as hot patches

## EM Cloud Control

Oracle Enterprise Manager Cloud Control 12c has a new patch management capability that reduces the difficulty and downtime associated with patching the database. The new patch management solution offers the following benefits:

- Integrated patching workflow with My Oracle Support. A single interface allows you to see recommendations, search for patches, and roll out patches.
- Patch plans allow for end-to-end orchestration of the patching workflow. Plans include including automated selection of deployment procedures and analysis of the patch conflicts.
- Easy review of patches for applicability to a given environment, validation of patch plans, and automatic receipt of patches to resolve validation issues.
- Deployable patch plans can be saved as patch templates, which contain a predetermined set of patches and deployment options.
- Out-of-place patching is possible for standalone database targets, Oracle Real Application Clusters (RAC) targets, and Oracle Grid Infrastructure targets.

Cloud Control patch plans help you create a consolidated list of patches you want to apply as a group to one or more targets. A patch can be added to a target in a plan only if the patch has the same release and platform as the target to which it is being added. The plan also validates Oracle Database, Fusion Middleware, and Cloud Control patches against the environment to check for conflicts with installed patches. Based on the patches added to it, Enterprise Manager automatically selects an appropriate deployment procedure to be used for applying the patches.

EM Cloud Control can apply patches in two different modes:

- **Online Mode** -- This mode is useful when Cloud Control can connect to My Oracle Support using an Internet connection. This mode allows administrators to see recommendations from Oracle for the patches to be applied, manually search patches directly on My Oracle Support and add them to a patch plan. It is also possible to automatically resolve patch conflicts with a merge patch directly from My Oracle Support.
- **Offline Mode** -- This mode is used when Cloud Control cannot connect to My Oracle Support. In this mode, it is only possible to search for patches that were manually uploaded to the Software Library, and add them to your patch plan.

**Queryable Patch Inventory**

Oracle 12c introduces a new feature called the Queryable Patch Inventory. This feature is implemented via the DBMS_QOPATCH package. It provides a PL/SQL or SQL interface to view the patches that are installed in the database. The interface provides all the patch information available as part of the OPatch lsinventory -xml command. DBMS_QOPATCH accesses the Oracle Universal Installer (OUI) patch inventory in real time to provide patch and patch meta information. With this feature, it is possible to:

- Query what patches are installed from a SQL prompt.
- Create reports and perform validation checks across multiple environments.
- Check patches installed on Oracle RAC nodes from a single location.

The subprograms available in the DBMS_QOPATCH include:

- **GET_OPATCH_BUGS** -- Provides a bugs list for a patch in XML format if the patch number is given. If patch is not given then it lists all the bugs installed in all the patches in XML format.
- **GET_OPATCH_COUNT** -- Provides the total number of installed patches in XML format.
- **GET_OPATCH_DATA** -- Provides top level patch information for the patch (such as Patch ID, patch creation time) in the XML element.
- **GET_OPATCH_FILES** -- Provides the list of files modified in the given patch number in XML format.
- **GET_OPATCH_INSTALL_INFO** -- Returns the XML element containing the ORACLE_HOME details such as patch and inventory location.
- **GET_OPATCH_LIST** -- Provides list of patches installed as an XML element from the XML inventory.
- **GET_OPATCH_LSINVENTORY** -- Returns whole opatch inventory as XML instance document.
- **GET_OPATCH_OLAYS** -- Provides overlay patches for a given patch as XML element.
- **GET_OPATCH_PREQS** -- Provides prerequisite patches for a given patch as XML element.
- **GET_OPATCH_XSLT** -- Returns the style-sheet for the opatch XML inventory presentation.
- **GET_PENDING_ACTIVITY** -- Returns the information related to SQL patches applied on a single instance by querying the binary inventory.
- **GET_SQLPATCH_STATUS** -- Displays the SQL patch status by querying from SQL patch registry to produce complete patch level information.
- **IS_PATCH_INSTALLED** -- Provides information (such as patchID, application date, and SQL patch information) on the installed patch as XML node by querying the XML inventory
- **PATCH_CONFLICT_DETECTION** -- Returns the conflicting patch for a given file, if it conflicts with an existing patch
- **SET_CURRENT_OPINST** -- Sets the node name and instance to get the inventory details specific to it in an Oracle Real Application Clusters (RAC) environment

# Back up and recover the database

The scope of backup and recovery is huge and cannot be covered in a single chapter. The following is no more than a brief overview of configuring Oracle's Recovery Manager (RMAN), creating backups, and recovering the database. You should reference the Backup and Recovery User's Guide for more details.

RMAN has a number of different settings to control the specific actions taken during backups. The default settings for most of these parameters make sense for performing standard backup and recovery operations. Understanding what these parameters are will allow you to optimize the behavior for a given database. Persistent settings can be set for each target database, such as backup destinations, device type, and retention policy. The two commands of interest for this purpose are:

- **SHOW** -- This command displays the current value of settings configured for RMAN in the target database. The command will indicate whether or not the current values are set to their default. This information is also available in the V$RMAN_CONFIGURATION view.
- **CONFIGURE** -- This command allows you to change RMAN current behavior for your backup and recovery environment. If used with the keyword CLEAR, this command will reset the parameter to the default RMAN value. Some examples of the options that can be set follow:

The following command sets the backup retention policy to maintain three full or level 0 backups of each data file and control file. Any backups older than the third file are considered obsolete. The default value is 1.

```
CONFIGURE RETENTION POLICY TO REDUNDANCY 3;
```

Alternately, the retention policy can be given a recovery window that ensures sufficient backups are kept to recover the database to any point in time back to the supplied value:

```
CONFIGURE RETENTION POLICY TO RECOVERY WINDOW OF 7 DAYS;
```

When a destination device type is not specific for a backup, RMAN sends it to whatever device type is configured as the default. RMAN is preset to use disk as the default device type. The following command allows you to change the default device type to tape:

```
CONFIGURE DEFAULT DEVICE TYPE TO sbt;
```

Regardless of the default device type, you can specifically direct a backup to a specific device type using the DEVICE TYPE clause of the BACKUP command, as shown in the following examples:

```
BACKUP DEVICE TYPE SBT DATABASE;
BACKUP DEVICE TYPE DISK DATABASE;
```

When backing up to disk, RMAN can be configured to create either backup sets or image copies by default (the backup type for tape can only be a backup set). In addition, RMAN can create backup sets using binary compression. Specifying the COMPRESSED option in the BACKUP TYPE TO ... BACKUPSET clause configures RMAN to use compressed backup sets by default for a given device type. Omitting the COMPRESSED keyword, disables compression. The preconfigured backup type for disk is an uncompressed backup set. The following examples show configuring RMAN backups to copies and backup sets:

```
CONFIGURE DEVICE TYPE DISK BACKUP TYPE TO BACKUPSET;
CONFIGURE DEVICE TYPE DISK BACKUP TYPE TO COPY;
```

To enable compression on backupsets, you would add the COMPRESSED keyword:

```
CONFIGURE DEVICE TYPE DISK BACKUP TYPE TO COMPRESSED BACKUPSET;
CONFIGURE DEVICE TYPE SBT BACKUP TYPE TO COMPRESSED BACKUPSET;
```

An RMAN channel is a connection to a database server session. The CONFIGURE CHANNEL command is used to configure options for disk or SBT channels. When the CONFIGURE CHANNEL command is used to specify default channel settings for a device, any previous settings are lost. Any settings not specified in the CONFIGURE CHANNEL command will be returned to their default value.

```
CONFIGURE CHANNEL DEVICE TYPE DISK MAXPIECESIZE 1G;
CONFIGURE CHANNEL DEVICE TYPE DISK FORMAT /tmp/%U;
```

RMAN allocates a single disk channel for all operations by default. You can change the default location and format for the file name for that channel. Be aware that when an explicit format is configured for disk channels, RMAN does not create backups by default in the fast recovery area.

```
CONFIGURE CHANNEL DEVICE TYPE DISK FORMAT '/u01/ora_df%t_s%s_s%p';
CONFIGURE CHANNEL DEVICE TYPE DISK FORMAT '+dgroup1';
```

It is possible to spread a backup across multiple hard drives. You must allocate a channel of DEVICE TYPE DISK for each disk drive and specify the format string.

```
RUN
{
  ALLOCATE CHANNEL U01 DEVICE TYPE DISK FORMAT '/u01/%U';
  ALLOCATE CHANNEL U02 DEVICE TYPE DISK FORMAT '/u02/%U';
  BACKUP DATABASE PLUS ARCHIVELOG;
}
```

RMAN can be set to automatically back up the control file and server parameter file whenever a backup record is added. In addition, if the database structure metadata in the control file changes and the database is in ARCHIVELOG mode, an autobackup will be taken. Control file autobackup adds additional redundancy to the recovery strategy, allowing RMAN to recover the database even after the loss of the current control file, recovery catalog, and server parameter file. The autobackup feature is enabled and disabled as follows:

```
CONFIGURE CONTROLFILE AUTOBACKUP ON;
CONFIGURE CONTROLFILE AUTOBACKUP OFF;
```

The RMAN configuration settings can be returned to their default values by using the CLEAR keyword:

```
CONFIGURE DEFAULT DEVICE TYPE CLEAR;
CONFIGURE RETENTION POLICY CLEAR;
CONFIGURE CONTROLFILE AUTOBACKUP CLEAR;
```

When RMAN backup optimization is enabled, RMAN will skip files during a backup operation if the identical file has already been backed up to the currently specified device type. In order to determine of the file is truly identical, RMAN uses the following criteria:

- **Datafile** --The datafile must have the same DBID, checkpoint SCN, creation SCN, and RESETLOGS SCN and time as a datafile already in a backup. The datafile must be offline-normal, read-only, or closed normally.
- **Archived log** -- The log must have the same DBID, thread, sequence number, and RESETLOGS SCN and time
- **Backup set** -- The backup set must have the same DBID, backup set record ID, and stamp.

Even if RMAN determines that the file is identical to one that has already been backed up, the retention policy or the backup duplexing feature may require it to be backed up. Also, if the TO DESTINATION is used in conjunction with BACKUP RECOVERY AREA or BACKUP RECOVERY FILES, RMAN will only look for identical backups in the specific TO DESTINATION location provided. Backup optimization is enabled by issuing the following command:

```
CONFIGURE BACKUP OPTIMIZATION ON;
```

Once backup optimization has been configured for a target database, if none of the backed-up files specified for a given job has changed since the last backup, then RMAN will not back up the files again. Even if every file for a given backup is skipped because the files have already been backed up, no error will occur. Backup optimization can be overridden by including the FORCE keyword in the BACKUP command:

```
BACKUP DATABASE FORCE;
BACKUP ARCHIVELOG ALL FORCE;
```

## Creating Backups

When RMAN creates image copies, the result is bit-for-bit copies of each data file, archived redo log file, or control file. Images copies can be used as-is to perform recovery. They are generated with the RMAN BACKUP AS COPY command, an operating system command such as the UNIX cp, or by the Oracle archiver process. The default RMAN backup type can be set to image using the CONFIGURE DEVICE TYPE COMMAND:

```
CONFIGURE DEVICE TYPE DISK BACKUP TYPE TO COPY;
```

It is also possible to override the default with the AS COPY clause of the BACKUP command:

```
BACKUP AS COPY
   DEVICE TYPE DISK
   DATABASE;
```

The other format type is backup sets. Backup sets consist of one or more data files, control files, server parameter files, and archived redo log files. Each backup set consists of one or more binary files. Each binary file is called a backup piece. Backup pieces are written in a proprietary format that can only be created or restored by RMAN. The contents of a backup set are divided among multiple backup pieces only if the backup piece size is limited using MAXPIECESIZE. This keyword is an option of the ALLOCATE CHANNEL or CONFIGURE CHANNEL command. As with image copies, the default type is set with the CONFIGURE DEVICE TYPE command:

```
CONFIGURE DEVICE TYPE DISK BACKUP TYPE TO BACKUPSET;
```

The default can be overridden using the AS BACKUPSET clause. You can allow backup sets to be created on the configured default device, or direct them specifically to disk or tape.

```
BACKUP AS BACKUPSET
   DATABASE;
```

```
BACKUP AS BACKUPSET
   DEVICE TYPE DISK
   DATABASE;
```

A whole database backup includes a backup of the control file and all data files that belong to a database. A whole database backup can be made with the database mounted or open. The RMAN command BACKUP DATABASE is used to perform a whole database backup.

```
BACKUP DATABASE;
```

Adding the PLUS ARCHIVELOGS clause will back up the database, switch the online redo logs, and include archived logs in the backup. This guarantees that you have the full set of archived logs through the time of the backup and guarantees that you can perform media recovery after restoring this backup.

```
BACKUP DATABASE PLUS ARCHIVELOG;
```

## Incremental Backups

The RMAN BACKUP INCREMENTAL command creates an incremental backup of a database. Incremental backups capture block-level changes to a database made after a previous incremental backup. Recovery with incremental backups is faster than using redo logs alone. There are three types of incremental backups:

- **Level 0** -- This is the starting point for an incremental backup. It backs up all blocks in the database and is identical in content to a full backup.
- **Level 1 Differential** -- This backup contains only blocks changed since the most recent incremental backup. This is the default Level 1 backup.
- **Level 1 Cumulative** -- This backup contains only blocks changed since the most recent level 0 backup.

When restoring incremental backups, RMAN uses the level 0 backup as the starting point. It then uses the level 1 backups to update changed blocks where possible to avoid reapplying changes from redo one at a time. If incremental backups are available, then RMAN uses them during recovery.

The following example creates a level 0 incremental backup to serve as a base for an incremental backup strategy:

```
BACKUP INCREMENTAL LEVEL 0 DATABASE;
```

The following example creates a level 1 cumulative incremental backup:

```
BACKUP INCREMENTAL LEVEL 1 CUMULATIVE DATABASE;
```

The following example creates a level 1 differential incremental backup:

```
BACKUP INCREMENTAL LEVEL 1 DATABASE;
```

## Block Change Tracking

The block change tracking feature improves backup performance for incremental backups by recording changed blocks for each data file. If block change tracking is enabled, RMAN uses a block change tracking file to identify changed blocks during incremental backups. This file keeps RMAN from having to scan every block in the data file that it is backing up. Block change tracking is disabled by default. A single block change tracking file is created for the whole database. By default, the change tracking file is created as an Oracle managed file in the destination specified by the DB_CREATE_FILE_DEST initialization parameter. A block change tracking file is only used when the incremental level is greater than 0, because a level 0 incremental backup includes all blocks. Once the file has been created and a level 0 incremental backup has been created, the next incremental backup can make use of the change tracking data. To enable block change tracking, execute the following ALTER DATABASE statement:

```
ALTER DATABASE ENABLE BLOCK CHANGE TRACKING;
```

You can also create the change tracking file in a specific location:

```
ALTER DATABASE ENABLE BLOCK CHANGE TRACKING
USING FILE '/ocpdir/rman_change_track.f' REUSE;
```

You can disable block change tracking by executing the following command:

```
ALTER DATABASE DISABLE BLOCK CHANGE TRACKING;
```

**Recovering the database**

The scope of performing a database recovery is enormous and depends on dozens of factors. However, the exam is unlikely to get into a hugely complex recovery scenario. This section makes the following assumptions:

- Some or all data files have been lost, but the database has not lost all current control files or an entire online redo log group.
- The database is using the current server parameter file.
- The complete set of archived redo logs and incremental backups needed for recovery of the data file backups are available. Every data file either has a backup, or a complete set of online and archived redo logs goes back to the creation of a data file with no backup.
- An encrypted tablespace is not part of the recovery.
- The database runs in a single-instance configuration.
- The database uses a fast recovery area.

To restore and recover the whole database:

- Start RMAN and connect to a target database.
  ```
  % rman
  RMAN> CONNECT TARGET /
  ```

- If the database is not mounted, then mount but do not open the database.
  ```
  STARTUP MOUNT;
  ```

- Use the SHOW command to see which channels are preconfigured.
  ```
  SHOW ALL;
  ```

  If the necessary devices and channels are already configured, then no action is necessary. Otherwise, you can use the CONFIGURE command to configure automatic channels, or include ALLOCATE CHANNEL commands within a RUN block.

- **Restore and recover the database.**
  ```
  RMAN> RESTORE DATABASE;
  Starting restore at 20-JAN-14
    .
    .
    .
  Finished restore at 20-JAN-14

  RMAN> RECOVER DATABASE;

  Starting recover at 20-JAN-14
    .
    .
    .
  media recovery complete, elapsed time: 00:00:21
  Finished recover at 20-JAN-14
  ```

- **Examine the output to see if media recovery was successful. If so, open the database.**
  ```
  ALTER DATABASE OPEN;
  ```

# Troubleshoot network and database issues

The first step in diagnosing any problem is to gather information about what went wrong. Each server and background process of Oracle can write to an associated trace file. When an internal error is detected by a process, it dumps information about the error to its trace file. Some of the information written to a trace file is intended for the database administrator, and other information is for Oracle Support Services.

In addition, all Oracle databases maintain an alert log file. The filename is in the form alert_<sid>.log  and it will be stored by default in the $ORACLE_BASE/diag/rdbms/<db_name>/<sid>/trace directory. The alert log is a chronological log of messages and errors regarding the database.

The file includes the following items:

- All internal errors (ORA-00600), block corruption errors (ORA-01578), and deadlock errors (ORA-00060) that occur
- Administrative operations, such as CREATE, ALTER, and DROP statements and STARTUP, SHUTDOWN, and ARCHIVELOG statements
- Messages and errors relating to the functions of shared server and dispatcher processes
- Errors occurring during the automatic refresh of a materialized view
- The values of all initialization parameters that had nondefault values at the time the database and instance start

The alert log records this information in lieu of displaying the information on the console (although some of these errors might also appear on-screen). Whenever one of the logged operations is successful, a "completed" message and timestamp are written to the alert log. There are two versions of the log maintained: an XML-formatted file and a text-formatted file. Either format of the alert log can be viewed with a text editor. Alternately, you can use the ADRCI command-line utility to view the XML-formatted version of the file. You should periodically check the alert log and trace files of an instance for errors that require intervention. Background processes always write to a trace file when appropriate. For the ARCn background process an initialization parameter can be used to control the amount and type of trace information that is produced. However, the other background processes have no such control capability. Trace files are written for server processes when critical errors occur.

Since the Oracle 11g release, all diagnostic files such as traces, dumps, the alert log, health monitor reports, and more are stored in a directory structure known as the Automatic Diagnostic Repository (ADR). The ADR structure supports multiple instances and multiple Oracle products. Each instance of each product will store diagnostic data underneath its own home directory within the ADR. ADR provides a unified directory structure along with consistent diagnostic data formats across products and instances. This plus a unified set of tools enables diagnostic data to be correlated and analyzed across multiple Oracle products.

The DIAGNOSTIC_DEST parameter identifies the directory which serves as the ADR Base location. To determine the locations of trace files, you can query the V$DIAG_INFO view:

```
SELECT name, value
FROM   v$diag_info
WHERE  name LIKE 'Diag%';

NAME            VALUE
-------------   ------------------------------------------
Diag Enabled    TRUE
Diag Trace      /u01/app/oracle/diag/rdbms/orcl/orcl/trace
Diag Alert      /u01/app/oracle/diag/rdbms/orcl/orcl/alert
Diag Incident   /u01/app/oracle/diag/rdbms/orcl/orcl/incident
Diag Cdump      /u01/app/oracle/diag/rdbms/orcl/orcl/cdump
```

Some of the locations in the V$DIAG_INFO view include:

- **ADR Base** – Path of ADR base.
- **ADR Home** – Path of ADR home for the current database instance.
- **Diag Trace** – Location of background process trace files, server process trace files, SQL trace files, and the text-formatted version of the alert log.
- **Diag Alert** – Location of the XML-formatted version of the alert log.
- **Default Trace** – File Path to the trace file for the current session.
- **Diag Incident** – File path for incident packages.
- **Diag Cdump** – Equivalent to cdump. Location for core dump files.
- **Health Monitor** – Location for health monitor output.

The fault diagnosability infrastructure is based on problems and incidents. A problem is defined as a critical error in the database. Critical errors manifest as internal errors, such as ORA-00600, ORA-07445, or ORA-04031. Problems are tracked in the ADR using a problem key, which is a text string that describes the problem.

An incident is defined as a single occurrence of a problem. When a problem occurs multiple times, an incident is created for each occurrence. Oracle timestamps the incidents and tracks them in the ADR. Incidents are identified by a numeric incident ID, which is unique within the ADR. Each incident in the database generates the following actions:

- An entry is made in the alert log.
- An incident alert is sent to Oracle Enterprise Manager.
- Diagnostic data about the incident is stored in the form of dump files.
- One or more incident dumps are stored in the ADR in a subdirectory created for that incident.

## Detect and repair data failures with Data Recovery Advisor

Oracle's Data Recovery Advisor is a data corruption repair function integrated with Support Workbench, database health checks and RMAN. It can display data corruption problems, assess their extent and impact, recommend repair options, and automate the repair process. In the context of Data Recovery Advisor, a health check is a diagnostic procedure run by the Health Monitor to assess the state of the database or its components. Health checks are invoked reactively when an error occurs and can also be invoked manually. Data Recovery Advisor can diagnose failures such as the following:

- Components such as data files and control files that are not accessible by the database.
- Physical corruptions such as block checksum failures and invalid block header field values.
- Inconsistencies such as a data file that is older than other database files.
- I/O failures such as hardware errors, operating system driver failures, and exceeding operating system resource limits.

In some cases, the Data Recovery Advisor may be able to detect or handle logical corruptions. As a general rule, detecting and repairing logical corruptions will require assistance from Oracle Support Services.

## Failures

A failure is a persistent data corruption detected by a health check. They are usually detected reactively when a database operation encounters corrupted data and generates an error. This will automatically invoke a health check in the database. The check will search the database for failures related to the error and record any findings in the Automatic Diagnostic Repository. Data Recovery Advisor can generate repair advice and repair failures only after failures have been detected by the database and stored in the ADR. Data Recovery Advisor can report on and repair failures such as inaccessible files, physical and logical block corruptions, and I/O failures. All failures are assigned a priority: CRITICAL, HIGH, or LOW, and a status of OPEN or CLOSED.

- **CRITICAL** priority failures require immediate attention because they make the whole database unavailable. Typically, critical failures bring down the instance and are diagnosed during the subsequent startup.
- **HIGH** priority failures make a database partially unavailable or unrecoverable, and usually have to be repaired in a reasonably short time.
- **LOW** priority indicates that failures can be ignored until more important failures are fixed.

## DRA Repairs

Data Recovery Advisor allows you to view repair options. Repairs might involve the use of block media recovery, datafile media recovery, or Oracle Flashback Database. In general, Data Recovery Advisor presents both automated and manual repair options. If appropriate, you can choose an automated repair option in order to perform a repair. In an automated repair, Data Recovery Advisor performs the repair, verifies the repair success, and closes the relevant failures.

The recommended workflow for repairing data failures from RMAN is to run the following commands in sequence during an RMAN session: LIST FAILURE to display failures, ADVISE FAILURE to display repair options, and REPAIR FAILURE to fix the failures.

## LIST FAILURE

The LIST FAILURE command displays failures against which you can run the ADVISE FAILURE and REPAIR FAILURE commands.

```
RMAN> LIST FAILURE;
List of Database Failures
=========================
Failure ID Priority Status  Time Detected Summary
---------- -------- ------- ------------- ----------------------
274        HIGH     OPEN    21-FEB-14     One or more non-system
                                          datafiles are missing
329        HIGH     OPEN    21-FEB-14     Datafile 1:
                                          '/u01/oradata/prod/
                                           system01.dbf'
                                          contains one or more
                                          corrupt blocks
```

## ADVISE FAILURE

Use the ADVISE FAILURE command to display repair options for the specified failures. This command prints a summary of the failures identified by the Data Recovery Advisor and implicitly closes all open failures that are already fixed. The ADVISE FAILURE command indicates the repair strategy that Data Recovery Advisor considers optimal for a given set of failures. Data Recovery Advisor verifies repair feasibility before proposing a repair strategy. For example, it will check that all backups and archived redo log files needed for media recovery are available. It can generate both manual and automated repair options.

The ADVISE command maps a set of failures to the set of repair steps that Data Recovery Advisor considers to be optimal. When possible, Data Recovery Advisor consolidates multiple repair steps into a single repair. For example, if the database has corrupted datafile, missing control file, and lost current redo log group, then Data Recovery Advisor would recommend a single, consolidated repair plan to restore the database and perform point-in-time recovery.

```
RMAN> ADVISE FAILURE;
List of Database Failures
=========================

Failure ID Priority Status Time Detected Summary
---------- -------- ------ ------------- ----------------------
274        HIGH     OPEN   21-FEB-14     One or more non-system
                                         datafiles are missing
329        HIGH     OPEN   21-FEB-14     Datafile 1:
                                         '/u01/oradata/prod/
                                         system01.dbf'
                                         contains one or more
                                         corrupt blocks

analyzing automatic repair options; this may take some time
using channel ORA_DISK_1
analyzing automatic repair options complete

Mandatory Manual Actions
=========================
no manual actions available

Optional Manual Actions
=========================
1. If file /u01/oradata/prod/data01.dbf was unintentionally renamed
or moved, restore it

Automated Repair Options
=========================
Option Repair Description
------ -------------------------------------------
Restore and recover datafile 31; Perform block
    media recovery of block 43481 in file 1

Strategy: The repair includes complete media recovery with no data
loss
Repair script:
/u01/oracle/log/diag/rdbms/prod/prod/hm/reco_740113269.hm
```

## CHANGE FAILURE

The CHANGE FAILURE command allows you to change the failure priority from HIGH to LOW or the reverse, or to close it. You cannot change to or from CRITICAL priority.

```
RMAN> CHANGE FAILURE 3 PRIORITY LOW;
```

## REPAIR FAILURE

The REPAIR FAILURE command is used to repair database failures identified by the Data Recovery Advisor. The target database instance must be started, it must be a single-instance database and cannot be a physical standby database. It is important that at most one RMAN session is running the REPAIR FAILURE command. The only exception is REPAIR FAILURE ... PREVIEW, which is permitted in concurrent RMAN sessions. To perform an automated repair, the Data Recovery Advisor may require specific backups and archived redo logs. If the files are not available, then the recovery will not be possible. Data Recovery Advisor consolidates repairs whenever possible so that a single repair can fix multiple failures. If one has not yet been issued in the current RMAN session, REPAIR FAILURE performs an implicit ADVISE FAILURE. RMAN always verifies that failures are still relevant and automatically closes failures that have already been repaired. After executing a repair, RMAN reevaluates all open failures on the chance that some of them may also have been fixed.

# Implement Flashback Technology
## Flashback Table

By default, when a table is dropped, the database does not immediately remove the space associated with the table. Instead, the database renames it and places the table and any associated objects that were dropped in a recycle bin. If it is determined that the table was dropped in error, it can be recovered at a later date. The FLASHBACK TABLE statement is used to restore the table.

The recycle bin is a data dictionary table that contains information required to recover dropped objects. The dropped objects themselves remain where they were before being dropped and still occupy the same amount of disk space. Dropped objects also continue to count against user space quotas until they are explicitly purged or are purged by the database due to tablespace space constraints.

When a tablespace including its contents is dropped, the recycle bin does not come into play. The storage where the objects were does not exist anymore. The database purges any entries in the recycle bin for objects that were located in the tablespace. If the recycle bin is disabled, dropped tables and their dependent objects are not placed in the recycle bin; they are just dropped. They must be recovered by other means, such as recovering from backup. The recycle bin is enabled by default.

The FLASHBACK TABLE ... TO BEFORE DROP statement is used to recover objects from the recycle bin. When recovering a table, you must specify either the system-generated name of the table in the recycle bin or the original table name. An optional RENAME TO clause lets you rename the table as you recover it. The USER_RECYCLEBIN view can be used to obtain the system-generated name. To use the FLASHBACK TABLE ... TO BEFORE DROP statement, you need the same privileges required to drop the table.

The following example restores ocp_employees table and assigns to it a new name:

```
FLASHBACK TABLE ocp_employees TO BEFORE DROP
RENAME TO ocp_employees_take2;
```

## Flashback Version Query

Flashback Version Query is used to retrieve metadata and historical data for a specific interval. The interval can be specified by two timestamps or by two SCNs. The metadata returned includes the start and end time a version existed, type of DML operation used to create it, and the identity of the transaction that created each row version. The VERSIONS BETWEEN clause of a SELECT statement is used to generate a Flashback Version Query. The syntax of the VERSIONS BETWEEN clause is:  VERSIONS {BETWEEN {SCN | TIMESTAMP} start AND end}.

The pseudocolumns returned by a Flashback version query are:

- **VERSIONS_START[SCN/TIME]** -- Starting System Change Number (SCN) or TIMESTAMP when the row version was created. NULL if version is from before the start value.
- **VERSIONS_END[SCN/TIME]** -- SCN or TIMESTAMP when the row version expired. If NULL, then either the row version was current at the time of the query or the row is for a DELETE operation.
- **VERSIONS_XID** -- Identifier of the transaction that created the row version.
- **VERSIONS_OPERATION** -- Operation performed by the transaction: I for insertion, D for deletion, or U for update. The version is that of the row that was inserted, deleted, or updated.

A given row version is valid starting at VERSIONS_START* up to, but not including, VERSIONS_END*. That is, it is valid for any time 't' such that VERSIONS_START* <= t < VERSIONS_END*. The following three updates were issued against the EMPLOYEES table, with a pause in-between.

```
UPDATE employees SET salary = 97000
WHERE emp_last='McCoy';
UPDATE employees SET salary = 102000
WHERE emp_last='McCoy';
UPDATE employees SET salary = 105000
WHERE emp_last='McCoy';
COMMIT;
```

Then the following Flashback Versions query was run against employees:

```
SELECT versions_starttime, versions_endtime,
       versions_xid, versions_operation AS OP,
       salary
  FROM employees
  VERSIONS BETWEEN TIMESTAMP
      TO_TIMESTAMP('22-FEB-14 11.46.00PM','DD-MON-YY HH:MI:SSAM')
  AND TO_TIMESTAMP('22-FEB-14 11.52.00PM','DD-MON-YY HH:MI:SSAM')
  WHERE emp_last = 'McCoy';
```

| VERSIONS_STARTTIME | VERSIONS_ENDTIME | VERSIONS_XID | OP | SALARY |
|---|---|---|---|---|
| 22-FEB-14 11.51.08PM | | 09000900A9010000 | U | 105000 |
| 22-FEB-14 11.49.50PM | 22-FEB-14 11.51.08PM | 04001A003F010000 | U | 102000 |
| 22-FEB-14 11.49.02PM | 22-FEB-14 11.49.50PM | 03002100A2010000 | U | 97000 |
| | 22-FEB-14 11.49.02PM | | | 93500 |

From the results above, you see the three updates against the table, each increasing the salary column value. It's clear when each salary value started and ended (save the initial value for which the start time was outside the window, and the final value which is current (and therefore has no end time). You can use VERSIONS_XID with Oracle Flashback Transaction Query to locate the metadata for any of the three transactions. This will include the SQL required to undo the row change and the user responsible for the change.

**Flashback Transaction Query**

A Flashback Transaction Query is used to retrieve metadata and historical data for a single transaction or for all transactions in a supplied interval. The data is generated from the static data dictionary view FLASHBACK_TRANSACTION_QUERY. The Flashback Transaction Query creates a column UNDO_SQL. The SQL text in this field is the logical opposite of the DML operation performed by the transaction shown. The code from this field can usually reverse the original transaction within reason (e.g. a SQL_UNDO INSERT operation would be unlikely to insert a row back at the same ROWID from which it was deleted). As a general rule, Oracle Flashback Transaction Query is used in conjunction with an Oracle Flashback Version Query that provides transaction IDs.

```
SELECT operation, start_scn, commit_scn, logon_user
  FROM flashback_transaction_query
    WHERE xid = HEXTORAW('09000900A9010000');

OPERATION      START_SCN COMMIT_SCN LOGON_USER
------------   --------- ---------- ------------
UNKNOWN           393394     393463 OCPGURU
BEGIN             393394     393463 OCPGURU
```

The following statement uses Oracle Flashback Version Query as a subquery to associate each row version with the LOGON_USER responsible for the row data change.

```
SELECT xid, logon_user
  FROM flashback_transaction_query
    WHERE xid IN (
      SELECT versions_xid
      FROM employees VERSIONS BETWEEN TIMESTAMP
        TO_TIMESTAMP('22-FEB-14 11.40.00 PM',
                     'DD-MON-YY HH:MI:SS AM') AND
        TO_TIMESTAMP('22-FEB-14 11.56.00 PM',
                     'DD-MON-YY HH:MI:SS AM')
      );
```

You can use the DBMS_FLASHBACK.TRANSACTION_BACKOUT procedure to roll back a transaction and its dependent transactions while the database remains online. Transaction backout uses undo data to create and execute the compensating transactions to return the affected data to its original state. TRANSACTION_BACKOUT does not commit the DML operations that it performs as part of transaction backout. However, it does hold all the required locks on rows and tables in the right form to prevent other dependencies from entering the system. To make the transaction backout permanent, you must explicitly commit the transaction.

In order to configure a database for the Oracle Flashback Transaction Query feature, the database must be running in ARCHIVELOG mode. In addition, the database administrator must enable supplemental logging.

```
ALTER DATABASE ADD SUPPLEMENTAL LOG DATA;
```

To perform Oracle Flashback Query operations, the administrator must grant appropriate privileges to the user who will be performing them. For Oracle Flashback Query, the administrator can do either of the following:

- To allow access to specific objects during queries, grant FLASHBACK and SELECT privileges on those objects.
- To allow queries on all tables, grant the FLASHBACK ANY TABLE privilege.

For Oracle Flashback Transaction Query, the administrator will need to grant the SELECT ANY TRANSACTION privilege. To allow execution of undo SQL code retrieved by an Oracle Flashback Transaction, the administrator will need to grant: SELECT, UPDATE, DELETE, and INSERT privileges for the appropriate tables. Finally, the administrator will need to grant the user EXECUTE privileges on the DBMS_FLASHBACK Package.

**Flashback Database**

Oracle's Flashback Database feature allows you to set the database back to an earlier time in order to correct problems caused by logical data corruption or user errors within a designated time window. Flashback Database is much more efficient than performing a point-in-time recovery and does not require a backup and restore operation. Flashback Database is accessible through the RMAN command FLASHBACK DATABASE or the SQL statement FLASHBACK DATABASE.

To enable Flashback Database, the database must have a Fast Recovery Area configured and a flashback retention target set. This target specifies how far in the past it should possible to rewind the database. Flashback

Database uses its own logging mechanism, creating flashback logs and storing them in the fast recovery area. The database must be set up in advance to create flashback logs in order to take advantage of this feature. Once configured, at regular intervals, the database copies images of each altered block in every data file into the flashback logs. These block images can later be used to reconstruct the data file contents to any moment for which logs exist. In addition to the flashback logs, redo logs on disk or tape must be available for the entire time period spanned by the flashback logs. The range of SCNs for which there is currently enough flashback log data to support the FLASHBACK DATABASE command is called the flashback database window.

If the Fast Recovery Area does not contain sufficient space for recovery files such as archived redo logs and other backups needed for the retention policy, the database may delete the flashback logs starting from the earliest SCNs. The flashback retention target does not guarantee that Flashback Database is available for the full period. A larger Fast Recovery Area may be required in this case.

Flashback Database has the following limitations:

- It can only undo changes to a data file made by Oracle Database. It cannot be used to repair media failures, or recover from accidental deletion of data files.
- It cannot undo a shrink data file operation.
- If the database control file is restored from backup or re-created, all accumulated flashback log information is discarded.
- If you Flashback Database to a target time at which a NOLOGGING operation was in progress, block corruption is likely in the database objects and datafiles affected by the NOLOGGING operation.


A normal restore point simply assigns a restore point name to an SCN or specific point in time. It functions as an alias for this SCN. If you use flashback features or point-in-time recovery, the restore point name can be used instead of a time or SCN. Normal restore points eventually age out of the control file if not manually deleted, so they require no ongoing maintenance. The following commands support the use of restore points:

- RECOVER DATABASE and FLASHBACK DATABASE commands in RMAN
- FLASHBACK TABLE statement in SQL

A guaranteed restore point also serves as an alias for an SCN in recovery operations. However, guaranteed restore points never age out of the control file and must be explicitly dropped. It ensures that you can use Flashback Database to rewind a database to the restore point SCN, even if the generation of flashback logs is not enabled. When enabled, a guaranteed restore point enforces the retention of flashback logs all the way back in time to the guaranteed SCN.

In order to enable Flashback Database, you must first ensure the database instance is open or mounted. If the instance is mounted, then the database must be shut down cleanly unless it is a physical standby database.

1. Optionally, set the DB_FLASHBACK_RETENTION_TARGET to the length of the desired flashback window in minutes. The default is 1 day (1440 minutes).
2. Enable the Flashback Database feature for the whole database:

   ```
   ALTER DATABASE FLASHBACK ON;
   ```

3. Optionally, disable flashback logging for specific tablespaces.

To disable Flashback Database logging, you must issue the following command on a database instance that is either in mount or open state:

```
ALTER DATABASE FLASHBACK OFF;
```

Maintaining flashback logs does not impose significant overhead on a database instance. Changed blocks are written to the flashback logs at relatively infrequent, regular intervals, to limit processing and I/O overhead. Optimizing performance is primarily a matter of ensuring that the writes occur as fast as possible.

- Use a fast file system for your fast recovery area, preferably without operating system file caching.
- Configure enough disk spindles for the file system that holds the fast recovery area.
- If the storage system used to hold the fast recovery area does not have nonvolatile RAM, then try to configure the file system on striped storage volumes with a relatively small stripe size such as 128 KB.
- For large databases, set the initialization parameter LOG_BUFFER to at least 8 MB.

The basic steps to perform a Flashback Database operation are:

1. Start RMAN and connect to the database to be rewound.
2. Place the database into MOUNT status.

```
SHUTDOWN IMMEDIATE;
STARTUP MOUNT;
```

3. Execute the FLASHBACK DATABASE command.

```
FLASHBACK DATABASE TO SCN 42340948;
```

4. Open the database read-only in SQL*Plus and run queries to verify the database contents.

```
ALTER DATABASE OPEN READ ONLY;
```

5. If the data meets the requirements, shut down the database and open it using RESETLOGS:

```
SHUTDOWN IMMEDIATE;
STARTUP MOUNT;
ALTER DATABASE OPEN RESETLOGS;
```

# Load and Unload Data

The Oracle Data Pump utility is designed to provide high-speed movement of data and metadata from one database to another. It replaces the export/import functionality that existed in earlier releases of Oracle. Data Pump is made up of three distinct parts:

- **expdp and impdp** – These are command-line clients that use the procedures provided in the DBMS_DATAPUMP package to execute export and import commands. They accept parameters entered at the command line that enable the exporting and importing of data and metadata for a complete database or for subsets of a database.
- **DBMS_DATAPUMP** – Also known as the Data Pump API, this package provides a high-speed mechanism to move all or part of the data and metadata for a site from one database to another. DBMS_DATAPUMP can be used independently of the impdp and expdp clients.
- **DBMS_METADATA** – Also known as the Metadata API, this package provides a centralized facility for the extraction, manipulation, and re-creation of dictionary metadata. DBMS_METADATA can be used independently of the impdp and expdp clients.

Data Pump jobs use a master table, a master process, and worker processes to perform the work and keep track of progress:

- **Master Table** – A master table is used to track the progress within a job while the data and metadata are being transferred. It is implemented as a user table within the database. A user performing an impdp or expdp must have the CREATE TABLE system privilege for the master table to be created plus sufficient tablespace quota. The master table will have the same name as the job that created it. A Data Pump job cannot have the same name as an existing table or view in that schema. The information in the master table is used to restart a job.
- **Master process** – A master process is created for every Data Pump Export job and Data Pump Import job. It controls the entire job, including communicating with the clients, creating and

controlling a pool of worker processes, and performing logging operations.

- **Worker Process** – The master process allocates work to be executed to worker processes that perform the data and metadata processing within an operation. Data Pump can employ multiple worker processes, running in parallel, to increase job performance.

## Monitor a Data Pump job

It's possible to use the Data Pump Export and Import utilities to attach to a running job. When attached in logging mode, status about the job is automatically displayed during execution in real-time. When attached using interactive-command mode, it's possible to request the job status.

Optionally, a log file can be written during the execution of a job. It summarizes the progress of the job, lists any errors, and records the completion status. You can also determine job status or to get other information about Data Pump jobs, through the Data Pump views:

- **DBA_DATAPUMP_JOBS** – Identifies all active Data Pump jobs in the database, regardless of their state, on an instance (or on all instances for RAC). It also shows all Data Pump master tables not currently associated with an active job.
- **DBA_DATAPUMP_SESSIONS** – Identifies the user sessions that are attached to a Data Pump job. The information in this view is useful for determining why a stopped Data Pump operation has not gone away.
- **V$SESSION_LONGOPS** – Data Pump operations that transfer table data (export and import) maintain an entry indicating the job progress. The entry contains the estimated transfer size and is periodically updated to reflect the actual amount of data transferred.

The V$SESSION_LONGOPS columns that are relevant to a Data Pump job are as follows:

- **USERNAME** - job owner
- **OPNAME** - job name
- **TARGET_DESC** - job operation
- **SOFAR** - megabytes transferred thus far during the job
- **TOTALWORK** - estimated number of megabytes in the job
- **UNITS** - megabytes (MB)
- **MESSAGE** - a formatted status message of the form: 'job_name: operation_name : nnn out of mmm MB done'

The Data Pump Export utility is invoked using the expdp command. The actions performed by the export operation are defined by the parameters you specify. They can be supplied either on the command line or in a parameter file. Data Pump Export can be controlled using a command line, a parameter file, or an interactive-command mode.

- **Command-Line** – Enables you to specify most of the export parameters from the command line.
- **Parameter File** – Allows you to specify command-line parameters in a parameter file. The PARFILE parameter cannot be used in a parameter file, because parameter files cannot be nested.
- **Interactive-Command** – Displays an export prompt from which you can enter various commands. Some commands are specific to interactive-command mode.

Data Pump jobs manage the following types of files:

- **Dump files** – Contain the data and metadata being moved.
- **Log files** – Record the messages associated with an operation.
- **SQL files** – Record the output of a SQLFILE operation.
- **Data Files** – Files specified by the DATA_FILES parameter during a transportable import.

There are different expdp modes for unloading different portions of the database. The mode is specified using the appropriate parameter. The available modes are:

- **Full** – In a full database export, the entire database is unloaded. This mode requires the user performing the export to have the DATAPUMP_EXP_FULL_DATABASE role. Specified using the FULL parameter.
- **Schema** – This is the default export mode. If you have the DATAPUMP_EXP_FULL_DATABASE role, then you can provide a list of schemas to export. Otherwise you can export only your own schema. Specified using the SCHEMAS parameter.
- **Table** – In table mode, only a specified set of tables, partitions, and their dependent objects are unloaded. You must have the DATAPUMP_EXP_FULL_DATABASE role to export tables that are not in your own schema. Specified using the TABLES parameter.
- **Tablespace** – In tablespace mode, only the tables contained in a specified set of tablespaces are unloaded. If a table is unloaded, then its dependent objects are also unloaded. Privileged users get all tables. Unprivileged users get only the tables in their own schemas. Specified using the TABLESPACES parameter.
- **Transportable Tablespace** – In transportable tablespace mode, only the metadata for the tables (and their dependent objects) within a specified set of tablespaces is exported. The tablespace data files are copied in a separate operation. Specified using the TRANSPORT_TABLESPACES parameter.

**expdp Parameters**

The following parameters are applicable to expdp:

- **ATTACH** – Attaches the client session to an existing export job and automatically places you in the interactive-command interface.
- **CONTENT** – Enables you to filter what Export unloads: data only, metadata only, or both.
- **DIRECTORY** – Specifies the default location to which Export can write the dump file set and the log file.

- **DUMPFILE** – Specifies the names, and optionally, the directory objects of dump files for an export job.
- **ESTIMATE** – Specifies the method that Export will use to estimate how much disk space each table in the export job will consume (in bytes).
- **ESTIMATE_ONLY** – Instructs Export to estimate the space that a job would consume, without actually performing the export operation.
- **EXCLUDE** – Enables you to filter the metadata that is exported by specifying objects and object types to be excluded from the export operation.
- **FILESIZE** – Specifies the maximum size of each dump file.
- **FULL** – Specifies that you want to perform a full database mode export.
- **INCLUDE** – Enables you to filter the metadata that is exported by specifying objects and object types for the current export mode.
- **JOB_NAME** – Used to identify the export job in subsequent actions.
- **LOGFILE** – Specifies the name, and optionally, a directory, for the log file of the export job.
- **PARFILE** – Specifies the name of an export parameter file.
- **QUERY** – Allows you to specify a query clause that is used to filter the data that gets exported.
- **SCHEMAS** – Specifies that you want to perform a schema-mode export.
- **TABLES** – Specifies that you want to perform a table-mode export.
- **TABLESPACES** – Specifies a list of tablespace names to be exported in tablespace mode.
- **TRANSPORT_TABLESPACES** -- Specifies that you want to perform an export in transportable-tablespace mode. This parameter is used to specify a list of tablespace names for which object metadata will be exported from the source database into the target database.

## impdp Parameters

Many of the above parameters are also applicable to impdp. In addition, several of the more common impdp parameters are:

- **REUSE_DATAFILES** – Specifies whether the import job should reuse existing data files for tablespace creation.
- **SQLFILE** – Specifies a file into which all of the SQL DDL that Import would have executed, based on other parameters, is written.
- **STATUS** – Specifies the frequency at which the job status display is updated.
- **TABLE_EXISTS_ACTION** – Tells import what to do if the table it is trying to create already exists.
- **REMAP_DATAFILE** – Changes the name of the source data file to the target data file name in all SQL statements where the source data file is referenced.
- **REMAP_SCHEMA** – Loads all objects from the source schema into a target schema.
- **REMAP_TABLE** – Allows you to rename tables during an import operation.
- **REMAP_TABLESPACE** – Remaps all objects selected for import with persistent data in the source tablespace to be created in the target tablespace.

The following commands are applicable when using Interactive mode:

- **ADD_FILE** – Add additional dump files.
- **CONTINUE_CLIENT** – Exit interactive mode and enter logging mode.
- **EXIT_CLIENT** – Stop the import or export client session, but leave the job running.
- **KILL_JOB** – Detach all currently attached client sessions and terminate the current job.
- **PARALLEL** – Increase or decrease the number of active worker processes for the current job.
- **START_JOB** – Restart a stopped job to which you are attached.
- **STATUS** – Display detailed status for the current job and/or set status interval.
- **STOP_JOB** – Stop the current job for later restart.

## Network-based Data Pump operations

When the NETWORK_LINK parameter is used with impdp as part of an import operation, data is moved directly using SQL. A SELECT clause retrieves the data from the remote database using the network link supplied with the parameter. A corresponding INSERT clause inserts the data into the target database. No dump files are involved in the operation. When the NETWORK_LINK parameter is used with expdp as part of an export operation, data from the remote database is written to dump files on the target database. A 'Current User' database link is not supported for use with Data Pump. Only the following types of database links are supported:

- Public (both public and shared)
- Fixed user
- Connected user


There are some restrictions for operations performed using the NETWORK Link parameter:

- When using full transportable export, tables with LONG or LONG RAW columns that reside in administrative tablespaces (such as SYSTEM or SYSAUX) are not supported.
- When transporting a database over the network using full transportable export, auditing cannot be enabled for tables stored in an administrative tablespace (such as SYSTEM and SYSAUX) if the audit trail information itself is stored in a user-defined tablespace.
- The source and target databases can differ by no more than two versions. For example, if one database is Oracle Database 12c, then the other database must be 12c, 11g, or 10g.

## SQL*Loader

SQL*Loader is useful for loading data from non-Oracle databases. It has a very flexible data parsing engine that can handle a wide range of flat file formats when loading data. Essentially any database has the ability to export data to a flat file format. SQL*Load can then make use of these files to import the data into tables in an Oracle database. SQL*Loader can perform the following functions:

- Load data across a network if your data files are on a different system than the database.
- Load data from multiple data files during the same load session.
- Load data into multiple tables during the same load session.
- Specify the character set of the data.
- Selectively load data based on the record values.
- Manipulate data before loading it, using SQL functions.
- Generate unique sequential key values in specified columns.
- Use the operating system's file system to access the data files.
- Load data from disk, tape, or named pipe.
- Generate sophisticated error reports.
- Load arbitrarily complex object-relational data.
- Use secondary data files for loading LOBs and collections.
- Use conventional, direct path, or external table loads.

SQL*Loader can be used with or without a control file. Using a control file provides more control over the load operation. Simple load operations can be performed without specifying a control file. This is referred to as SQL*Loader express mode. SQL*Loader sessions make use of the following files:

- **Control** – Defines the format of the data file and controls the behavior of SQL*Loader.
- **Data** – One or more data files will contain the information to be loaded.
- **Log** – Contains a log of the actions performed by SQL*Loader and errors encountered.
- **Bad** – Contains all records that could not be loaded due to errors.

- **Discard** – Contains all records that the control file identified to be bypassed.

The sqlldr executable is used to invoke SQL*Loader. It is optionally followed by parameters that establish session characteristics. Parameters can also be specified using the following methods instead of the command line:

- Parameters can be added to a parameter file. To use a parameter file, the name of the file can be supplied in the command line using the PARFILE parameter.
- Some parameters can be specified within the SQL*Loader control file using the OPTIONS clause.

If the same parameter is specified on the command line and in a parameter file or OPTIONS clause, the value in the command line is used.

The SQL*Loader control file is a text file that tells SQL*Loader where to find the data file, the format to use in parsing the data, what table(s) to insert the data in to, and more. A control file has three loosely-defined sections:

- The first section contains session-wide information such as global options, the input data file location, and the data to be loaded.
- The second section consists of one or more INTO TABLE blocks. The blocks hold information about the destination table.
- The third section is optional and, if present, contains input data.

SQL*Loader has two methods of inserting data into Oracle tables, Conventional Path and Direct Load options. In conventional path, SQL*Loader effectively creates INSERT statements for the records in the file to be loaded and passes them to the Oracle SQL Parser to be handled. When using Direct Path, SQL*Loader bypasses SQL and the parser and loads data directly into the target table(s). Direct Path load is much faster, but Conventional Path is more flexible. Some restrictions of the Direct Path load are:

- It cannot run concurrently with other transactions against the target table.
- Triggers on the table do not fire.
- Data is written above the high-water mark of the table even if there is space below.
- Clustered tables are not supported.
- Foreign Key constraints are disabled during the load.

## Relocate SYSAUX occupants

The SYSAUX tablespace is an auxiliary tablespace to the SYSTEM tablespace. Some of the Oracle database components that formerly created and used separate tablespaces are now located in the SYSAUX tablespace by default. If the SYSAUX tablespace becomes unavailable, core database functionality will remain operational. The features that make use of objects in the SYSAUX tablespace may fail or continue to function with limited capability. The V$SYSAUX_OCCUPANTS view can be used to determine the occupants of the SYSAUX tablespace. The view lists the following information about the occupants:

- Name of the occupant
- Occupant description
- Schema name
- Move procedure
- Current space usage

The procedure displayed in the MOVE_PROCEDURE column of V$SYSAUX_OCCUPANTS allows the objects for that component to be moved out of the SYSAUX view. For a component that has been moved out of SYSAUX the same procedure can be used to move is back into the

SYSAUX tablespace. The following query shows a partial listing of database components, their description, and the procedure to move them from one tablespace to another:

```
SELECT occupant_name, occupant_desc, move_procedure
FROM    v$sysaux_occupants
WHERE   move_procedure IS NOT NULL;

OCCUPANT_NAME   OCCUPANT_DESC     MOVE_PROCEDURE
--------------  ----------------  -----------------------------------
LOGMNR          LogMiner          SYS.DBMS_LOGMNR_D.SET_TABLESPACE
LOGSTDBY        Logical Standby   SYS.DBMS_LOGSTDBY.SET_TABLESPACE
AUDIT_TABLES    DB audit tables   DBMS_AUDIT_MGMT.move_dbaudit_tables
XDB             XDB               XDB.DBMS_XDB.MOVEXDB_TABLESPACE
```

## Create a default permanent tablespace

It is possible to set a default permanent tablespace to be used for user accounts that have not been explicitly assigned a default tablespace. This feature was added to prevent the nasty alternative, which was newly-created users having their default permanent tablespace become SYSTEM when one was not assigned. Both the CREATE DATABASE and ALTER DATABASE statements have a DEFAULT TABLESPACE clause. The following example sets the default permanent tablespace to USERS:

```
ALTER DATABASE DEFAULT TABLESPACE users;
```

The current settings for the default tablespaces can be determined by querying the database_properties view:

```
SELECT property_name, property_value
FROM    database_properties
WHERE   property_name like '%TABLESPACE';

PROPERTY_NAME                     PROPERTY_VALUE
--------------------------------  --------------
DEFAULT_TEMP_TABLESPACE           TEMP2
DEFAULT_PERMANENT_TABLESPACE      USERS
```

When a default permanent tablespace is set (or changed) all objects created by users who do not have a default tablespace explicitly assigned will be created there unless the create statement explicitly references another tablespace.

## Use the Redo Logfile Size Advisor

The size of the redo logs in a given database can affect overall performance. The behavior of the DBW and ARCH processes are partially dependent on the redo log sizes. As a general rule, larger redo log files provide improved performance. When the log files are too small, this will increase checkpoint activity. The frequency of checkpointing is affected by several factors, including the side of the log files and the setting of the FAST_START_MTTR_TARGET initialization parameter. When the FAST_START_MTTR_TARGET parameter is set in order to reduced the instance recovery time, the Database automatically tries to checkpoint frequently enough to meet that target.

The optimal size for the log files can be obtained by querying the OPTIMAL_LOGFILE_SIZE column of the V$INSTANCE_RECOVERY view. This information is also available in the Redo Log Groups page of Oracle Enterprise Manager. As a rule of thumb, redo log files are generally in the range of 100 MB to a few gigabytes. They should be sized based on the amount of redo your system generates. Log files should switch at most once every twenty minutes as a rough approximation.

## Use Secure File LOBs

Starting with Oracle 11g, a new type of Large-Object storage was added to the Oracle database, SecureFile LOBs. The legacy LOB format was renamed to BasicFile LOBs. SecureFile LOBs add several new capabilities to LOB data storage:

- Intelligent LOB compression enables users to explicitly compress data to save disk space.
- Intelligent LOB encryption allows encrypted data to be stored in-place and is available for random reads and writes.
- The deduplication option allows Oracle to automatically detect duplicate LOB data and conserve space by only storing a single copy of the data.
- LOB data path optimization includes logical cache above storage layer, read prefetching, new caching modes, vectored IO, and more.

The init.ora parameter, db_securefile, is used to determine the behavior of the Oracle database in reference to using or not using SecureFile LOBs or BasicFile LOBs. The possible values of this parameter are: ALWAYS, FORCE, PERMITTED, NEVER, and IGNORE. The meaning of each of the values is:

- **ALWAYS** -- Attempt to create SecureFile LOBs but fall back to BasicFile LOBs if the tablespace is not using ASSM.
- **PERMITTED** -- Allow SecureFile LOBs to be created
- **PREFERRED** -- All LOBs are created as SecureFiles unless BASICFILE is explicitly specified in the LOB storage clause or the tablespace is a Manual Segment Space Management tablespace. When PREFERRED is set, cases where BASICFILE would otherwise be inherited from the partition or column level LOB storage are ignored; the LOBs will be created as SecureFiles instead.
- **NEVER** -- Disallow SecureFile LOBs from being created. If a DML statement tries to create a column as a SecureFile LOB, it will instead be created as a BasicFile LOB. If any SecureFile specific storage options or features are in the DML, an exception is created.
- **IGNORE** -- The SECUREFILE keyword and all SecureFiles options are ignored.

Online redefinition can be performed at the table or partition level. Using online redefinition means that the tables or partitions do not need to be taken offline. You can also perform the operation in parallel. However, the operation will require additional storage equal to the entire table or partition and all LOB segments. Also, after the migration, global indexes for the table will have to be rebuilt.

SecureFiles inherit the LOB column settings for deduplication, encryption, and compression that were specified at the time the LOB was created. There are several procedures in the DBMS_LOB package that allow you to determine or override the inherited values.

- **DBMS_LOB.GETOPTIONS** -- The current settings of a SecureFile LOB can be obtained using this function. An integer corresponding to a pre-defined constant based on the option type is returned. As an example, the value for DEDUPLICATE_OFF is 0. You won't need to know the values for the test. You might need to know the procedure name.
- **DBMS_LOB.SETOPTIONS** -- This procedure sets features of a SecureFile LOB (compression, deduplication, and encryption). It enables the features to be set on a per-LOB basis, overriding the default LOB settings.
- **DBMS_LOB.ISSECUREFILE** -- This function returns TRUE or FALSE depending on whether the LOB locator (BLOB or CLOB) passed to it is for a SecureFile.

The existing SPACE_USAGE procedure in the DBMS_SPACE package is overloaded to return information about LOB space usage. It returns the amount of disk space in blocks used by all the LOBs in the LOB segment. This procedure can only be used on tablespaces that are created with auto segment space management.

# Use Direct NFS

Starting with Oracle 11g, a native NFS client capability was imbedded as part of the Oracle Database kernel. This feature improves performance and manageability when using Network File System drives. The Direct NFS

Client improves I/O performance by incorporating Oracle-specific optimizations and eliminating the overhead from the operating system kernel NFS support. In addition, Direct NFS simplifies configuration by eliminating the need to manually tune most of the NFS parameters.

To use Direct NFS, the NFS file systems must first be mounted and available via the operating system kernel. Direct NFS does *not* mount the drives. The specific mount options used by the operating system aren't important, as Direct NFS Client manages Oracle's access to the drive. The Direct NFS Client will use either a new configuration file called 'oranfstab' or the mount tab file (/etc/mtab on Linux) to determine the mount point settings for NFS storage devices. Oracle first looks for the mount settings in $ORACLE_HOME/dbs/oranfstab, which would specify the Direct NFS Client settings for a single database. Second, Oracle looks for settings in /etc/oranfstab, which specifies the NFS mounts available to all Oracle databases on that host. Finally, Oracle reads the mount tab file (/etc/mtab on Linux) to identify available NFS mounts. If duplicate entries exist in the configuration files, Direct NFS Client will use the first entry found. In addition to populating one of these files with the NFS mount settings, you must replace the standard Oracle Disk Manager (ODM) library with one that supports Direct NFS Client. A sample oranfstab file would look similar to the following:

```
server: MyNFSServer1
path: 192.168.1.1
path: 192.168.1.2
path: 192.168.1.3
path: 192.168.1.4
export: /vol/oradata1 mount: /mnt/oradata1
```

Once the file exists, the following commands will enable the Direct NFS Client ODM Library

```
$ cd $ORACLE_HOME/lib
$ cp libodm11.so libodm11.so_stub
$ ln -s libnfsodm11.so libodm11.so
```

# Performance Management

## Design the database layout for optimal performance

If you put five Oracle DBAs in a room to discuss the proper file layout for optimal performance, the result will be six different opinions. That said, the 'right' answer in this case is the one that the OU test creators picked. One of the standard recommendations from Oracle when developing an I/O design plan is to use Oracle Automatic Storage Management (Oracle ASM). Because of the way in which Oracle ASM stripes data across all of the available disk groups, many of the rules for file layouts simply do not apply when using it. Oracle ASM provides the following capabilities:

- Striping
- Mirroring
- Online storage reconfiguration and dynamic rebalancing
- Managed file creation and deletion

For systems not using Automatic Storage Management, there are several possible configurations for optimizing disk performance, including:

- **Stripe Everything Across Every Disk** -- One of the simplest options to distribute I/O for minimizing contention is to build a single volume striped across all available disks. For recoverability, the volume would be mirrored (RAID 1).
- **Move Archive Logs to Different Disks** -- When the archived redo log files are stored on the same set of disks as other database files, I/O requests on those disks will be impacted when the database is archiving the redo logs. Moving these files to separate disks will improve the performance of the archive operation and ensure that nothing else is affected by the degraded response time on the archive destination disks.
- **Move Redo Logs to Separate Disks** -- In databases with a high level of update operations (OLTP systems in particular), the redo logs are write-intensive. Moving these files to disks separate from both the datafiles and the archived redo log files will mean that

writing redo logs is performed at the highest possible rate. Transaction processing performance will be maximized and writing the redo logs will not be impaired by any other I/O.

## Monitor performance

There are a significant number of tools and techniques for identifying performance issues. One of the easiest in recent releases of Oracle has been to use Enterprise Manager. In 12c, there is Enterprise Manager Cloud Control, Oracle's enterprise information technology management product. EM Cloud Control is designed to manage entire IT environments, including databases, server, middleware products and more. The kid brother of EM Cloud Control is EM Express.

EM Express is a web-based tool for managing Oracle Database 12c that is built into the database server. It is a lightweight tool designed to incur minimal overhead on the database server and provides the ability to perform basic administrative tasks as well as the ability to diagnose performance issues and tune the database. There are no background tasks or information-collecting processes associated with EM Express. The tool makes use of data that is already collected by the Oracle database. The Performance Hub of EM Express is going to be the 'go to' spot for many administrators in 12c for diagnosing performance issues. The image below shows the main page of the EM Express Performance Hub.

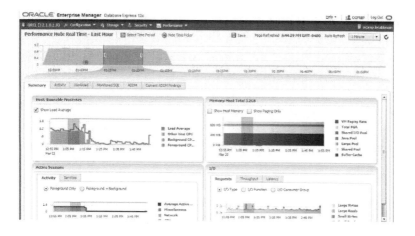

The Performance Hub provides a consolidated view of all performance data for a given time range. The performance data shown includes ASH Analytics, SQL Monitor, ADDM, as well as metrics that describe workload characteristics and database resource usage.

The Performance Hub can be used to view both historical and real-time data. A time range can be selected using a time picker at the top of the page, and the detail tabs will display the available performance data for the selected time range. The time picker displays average active sessions over time. When there are peaks in the time picker, the selected time range can be moved to the period of interest to gain more information.

When functioning in real-time mode, performance data is retrieved from in-memory views. The time picker shows data for the past hour and the user can select any time range from within this period. The default selection is the past 5 minutes. When functioning in historical mode, data is retrieved from the Automatic Workload Repository (AWR). The user can select any time period, provided there is sufficient data in AWR. The Performance Hub can also be saved as a Composite Active Report.

The Performance Hub organizes performance data by dividing it into different tabs that address a specific aspect of database performance. The tabs available in the Performance Hub are:

- **Summary** -- In real-time mode, this tab shows metrics data that gives an overview of system performance in terms of Host Resource Consumption (CPU, I/O and Memory), and Average Active Sessions. In historical mode, the tab displays system performance in terms of resource consumption, average active sessions, and load profile information.
- **Activity** -- Displays ASH Analytics in both real-time and historical mode.
- **Workload** -- Displays metric information about the workload profile, such as call rates, logon rate and the number of sessions. In addition, the tab also displays the Top SQL for the selected time range. In real-time mode, the tab displays Top SQL only by DB time. In historical mode, the user can also display Top SQL by other metrics, such as CPU time or Executions.
- **RAC** -- Displays RAC-specific metrics such as the number of global cache blocks received, and the average block latency when the database is in a RAC configuration.
- **Monitored SQL** -- Displays Monitored Executions of SQL, PL/SQL and Database Operations in both real-time and historical mode.
- **ADDM** -- Displays ADDM and Automatic Real Time ADDM reports in both real-time and historical mode.
- **Current ADDM Findings** -- Displays a real-time analysis of system performance for the past 5 minutes. The tab is available only in real-time mode and the contents of this tab are populated only if the time selector includes the current time.

## Manage memory

Once upon a time, tuning the various memory pools of an Oracle server was a very manual process and one that involved a fair amount of guesswork. Over the past several releases, Oracle has adding increasing amounts of automation to this process. With 12c, a single parameter allows the Database instance to automatically manage all of the memory pools. When the MEMORY_TARGET parameter is to a target memory size, the Oracle instance will grab this much memory on startup and allocate it automatically to the various memory pools.

Optionally you can specify a maximum memory size with the MEMORY_MAX_TARGET initialization parameter. The MEMORY_TARGET initialization parameter is dynamic and can be changed without restarting the database. The MEMORY_MAX_TARGET is not dynamic and requires a shutdown to change. It serves as an upper limit on the value assigned to the MEMORY_TARGET parameter so that you cannot accidentally set it too high.

When using Automatic memory management, the instance distributes memory between the SGA and PGA automatically. The instance dynamically redistributes memory between the two as memory requirements change. Databases created with DBCA using the basic installation option will have automatic memory management enabled by default. If a database is not currently using Automatic Memory Management, you can enable it using the following commands:

```
ALTER SYSTEM SET MEMORY_TARGET = nM;
ALTER SYSTEM SET SGA_TARGET = 0;
ALTER SYSTEM SET PGA_AGGREGATE_TARGET = 0;
```

Optionally you can issue the following command:

```
ALTER SYSTEM SET MEMORY_MAX_TARGET = nM SCOPE = SPFILE;
```

The relationships between the four parameters utilized by Automatic Memory Management are:

- **memory_target** – When MEMORY_TARGET is set, the database will allocate this much memory on startup, by default granting 60% to the SGA and 40% to the PGA. Over time, as the database runs, it will redistribute memory as needed between the system global area (SGA) and the instance program global area (instance PGA). If MEMORY_TARGET is not set, automatic memory management is not enabled, even if you have set a value for MEMORY_MAX_TARGET.
- **memory_max_target** – When set, this determines the maximum amount of memory that Oracle will grab from the OS for the SGA

and PGA. If this value is not set, it will default to the MEMORY_TARGET value.

- **sga_target** – This value is not required if using automatic memory management. If this value is set and MEMORY_TARGET is also set, then the value of SGA_TARGET becomes the minimum amount of memory allocated to the SGA by automatic memory management.
- **pga_aggregate_target** – This value is not required if using automatic memory management. If this value is set and MEMORY_TARGET is also set, then the value of PGA_AGGREGATE_TARGET becomes the minimum amount of memory allocated to the PGA by automatic memory management.

## Automatic Shared Memory Management

Automatic Shared Memory Management (ASMM) was the precursor to Automatic Memory Management (AMM). If you want to use ASMM instead of AMM, the total amount of SGA memory available to an instance is specified using the SGA_TARGET initialization parameter. Oracle will automatically distribute this memory among the various SGA components. When using ASMM, a few components of the SGA are still manually sized, including:

- **LOG_BUFFER** -- The log buffer.
- **DB_KEEP_CACHE_SIZE** -- The keep buffer cache.
- **DB_RECYCLE_CACHE_SIZE** -- The recycle buffer cache.
- **DB_nK_CACHE_SIZE** -- Nonstandard block size buffer caches

Any memory allocated to the manually-sized components is subtracted from the SGA_TARGET value and the remainder is allocated among the automatically Sized SGA Components:

- **SHARED_POOL_SIZE** -- The shared pool.
- **LARGE_POOL_SIZE** -- The large pool
- **JAVA_POOL_SIZE** -- The Java pool
- **DB_CACHE_SIZE** -- The buffer cache

- **STREAMS_POOL_SIZE** -- The Streams pool

The dynamic memory allocation functionality of both Automatic Memory Management and Automatic Shared Memory Management make use of statistics gathered for the database in allocating memory. For this reason, neither option can be used if the initialization parameter STATISTICS_LEVEL is set to BASIC.

## Buffer Cache

The database buffer cache is divided into one or more buffer pools. Separate buffer pools can be manually configured that either keep data in the buffer cache or make the buffers available for new data immediately after using the data blocks. Specific schema objects can be assigned to the appropriate buffer pool to provide more control over how blocks age out of the cache. The possible buffer pools are:

- **Default pool** -- This is where blocks are normally cached. Unless you manually configure separate pools, the default pool is the only buffer pool.
- **Keep pool** -- This is intended for blocks that are accessed frequently, but still get aged out of the default buffer pool due to other segments needing space. The goal of the keep buffer pool is to retain objects in memory longer to reduce I/O operations.
- **Recycle pool** -- This is intended for blocks that are used infrequently. A recycle pool prevents objects from consuming unnecessary space in the cache. This would be a place to assign large segments that are accessed very randomly. In the default pool, they would cause excessive buffer flushing with no benefit because by the time the block was needed again it would have been aged out of the cache.

## Analyze and identify performance issues

Automatic Database Diagnostic Monitor (ADDM) is a utility built into the Oracle database which automatically detects and reports performance problems. ADDM functionality is based on the snapshots taken by the Automatic Workload Repository (AWR). Data from the snapshots are analyzed and the results are displayed as ADDM findings on the Database Home page in Oracle Enterprise Manager Cloud Control. Cloud Control is the primary interface for diagnostic monitoring and whenever possible, you should run ADDM using it. If Cloud Control is unavailable, then it is also possible to run ADDM using the DBMS_ADDM package. In order to run the DBMS_ADDM APIs, the user must be granted the ADVISOR privilege.

ADDM findings allow administrators to quickly identify the performance problems affecting the database. Reviewing the findings of ADDM analysis should be one of the first steps in troubleshooting performance problems. Every ADDM finding will include one or more recommendations for reducing the impact of the performance problem. Regularly monitoring and implementing the recommendations from ADDM findings should be part of an administrator's routine maintenance process.

After each AWR snapshot is taken (hourly by default), an ADDM analysis is performed and the results saved in the database. If a potential performance problem is detected, ADDM then performs the following steps:

- Locates the root causes of the performance problem.
- Provides recommendations for correcting it.
- Quantifies the expected benefits.
- Identifies areas where no action is necessary.

ADDM analysis is performed from the top down. The utility identifies symptoms of performance issues and refines the analysis in an attempt to identify the root causes of the problem. ADDM uses the DB time statistic to identify performance problems. Database time is the cumulative time spent by the database in processing user requests. DB Time includes the wait time and CPU time of all non-idle user sessions. The ultimate goal is to minimize the DB time of the system for a given workload. This allows the database to service more user requests with a given set of resources.

Performance tuning is an iterative process. Any time one problem is resolved, another portion of the system may become a performance bottleneck. Resolving performance issues may take several cycles even with the benefit of the ADDM. When performance problems are identified, ADDM recommends potential solutions. If applicable, ADDM may recommend multiple solutions for a given problem. ADDM recommendations may include the following:

- **Hardware changes** -- Adding CPUs or changing the I/O subsystem configuration
- **Database configuration** -- Altering initialization parameter settings
- **Schema changes** – This could include hash partitioning a table or index, or using automatic segment space management (ASSM)
- **Application changes** – Examples might be using the cache option for sequences or using bind variables
- **Using other advisors** – This might include running SQL Tuning Advisor on high-load SQL statements or running the Segment Advisor on hot objects

ADDM is enabled in the database by default. It is controlled by the initialization parameters CONTROL_MANAGEMENT_PACK_ACCESS and STATISTICS_LEVEL. For ADDM to be enabled, CONTROL_MANAGEMENT_PACK_ACCESS should be set to DIAGNOSTIC+TUNING (default) or DIAGNOSTIC. Setting this parameter to NONE disables many Oracle Database features, including ADDM, and is strongly discouraged. The STATISTICS_LEVEL parameter should be set to TYPICAL (default) or ALL to enable ADDM. Setting this parameter to BASIC disables many Oracle Database features, including ADDM, and is strongly discouraged.

The analysis of I/O performance partially depends on the value of the DBIO_EXPECTED parameter. This parameter describes the expected performance of the I/O subsystem. The value is the average time in milliseconds that it takes to read a single database block. By default, Oracle uses a value of 10 milliseconds, which is appropriate for most hard drives. It is possible to choose a different value based on the characteristics of the hardware on the database server. If the appropriate value is determined to be different, it is possible to change the DBIO_EXPECTED value. The following statement will set DBIO_EXPECTED to 7000 microseconds when run as the SYS user:

```
EXECUTE DBMS_ADVISOR.SET_DEFAULT_TASK_PARAMETER('ADDM',
        'DBIO_EXPECTED', 7000);
```

The default settings for AWR are to generate snapshots of performance data once every hour, and retain the statistics in the workload repository for eight days. It is possible to change the default values for both the snapshot interval and the retention period. Oracle recommends that the retention period be set to at least one month. Longer periods may be advisable to span a full business cycle depending on the nature of the organization.

ADDM analysis results are represented as a set of findings. ADDM finding belongs to one of three classes:

- **Problem** -- Findings that describe the root cause of a database performance issue
- **Symptom** -- Findings that contain information that often leads to one or more problem findings
- **Information** -- Findings that are used to report areas of the system that do not have a performance impact

Every problem finding will be quantified with an estimate of the portion of DB time that resulted from it. If a problem has multiple causes, ADDM may report multiple findings for it. Recommendations are composed of actions and rationales. All actions of a given recommendation must be implemented in order to gain its estimated benefit. An ADDM action may present multiple solutions. If this is the case, then choose the easiest solution to implement.

# Perform real application testing

Real Application Testing makes use of two Oracle utilities, Database Replay and SQL Performance Analyzer (SPA). These two together provide a comprehensive testing solution for ensuring that planned changes to an Oracle database will not adversely affect application performance. SPA has the ability to assess the results of an environment change on SQL execution plans and statistics by running the SQL statements in isolation and serial manner in the current and planned environments. The SQL Performance Analyzer makes use of SQL Tuning Sets, SQL Tuning Advisor, and SQL Plan Management. It automates and simplifies the process of determining the potential impact of a change on even extremely large SQL workloads.

## SQL Performance Analyzer

Before running the SQL Performance Analyzer, you must capture the SQL statements from the system that you intend to analyze. Capturing a SQL workload has a negligible performance impact on a production system. Capturing a workload that contains large number SQL statements will better represent the production system database. This will assist SQL Performance Analyzer in accurately forecasting the potential impact of system changes. Ideally, you should capture all SQL statements that are either called by the application or are running on the production database. Captured SQL statements can be stored in a SQL tuning set and used as an input for SQL Performance Analyzer. A SQL tuning set is a database object that includes one or more SQL statements, along with their execution statistics and execution context.

SQL statements can be loaded into a SQL tuning set from many different sources. It's possible to use the cursor cache, Automatic Workload Repository (AWR), or existing SQL tuning sets. Using a SQL tuning set enables you to:

- Store the SQL text and any necessary auxiliary information in a single, persistent database object
- Populate, update, delete, and select captured SQL statements in the SQL tuning set
- Load and merge content from various data sources, such as the Automatic Workload Repository (AWR) or the cursor cache
- Export the SQL tuning set from the system where the SQL workload is captured and import it into another system
- Reuse the SQL workload as an input source for other advisors, such as the SQL Tuning Advisor and the SQL Access Advisor

**Views**

The following views allow you to monitor SQL Performance Analyzer and view its analysis results:

- The **DBA_ADVISOR_TASKS** view displays descriptive information about the SQL Performance Analyzer task that was created.
- The **DBA_ADVISOR_EXECUTIONS** view displays information about task executions.
- The **DBA_ADVISOR_FINDINGS** view displays the SQL Performance Analyzer findings. SQL Performance Analyzer generates the following types of findings:
  o Problems, such as performance regression
  o Symptoms, such as when the structure of an execution plan has changed
  o Errors, such as nonexistence of an object or view
  o Informative messages
- The **DBA_ADVISOR_SQLPLANS** view displays a list of all execution plans.
- The **DBA_ADVISOR_SQLSTATS** view displays a list of all SQL compilations and execution statistics.

- The **V$ADVISOR_PROGRESS** view displays the operation progress of SQL Performance Analyzer.

**Steps in analyzing performance changes**

- Capture the SQL workload that you intend to analyze and store it in a SQL tuning set.
- If you plan to use a test system separate from your production system, then the test system should be set up to match the production environment as closely as possible and the SQL tuning set must be transferred to the test system.
- On the test system, create a SQL Performance Analyzer task.
- Build the pre-change SQL trial by executing the SQL statements stored in the SQL tuning set.
- Perform the system change.
- Build the post-change SQL trial by re-executing the SQL statements in the SQL tuning set on the post-change test system.
- Compare and analyze the pre-change and post-change versions of performance data, and generate a report to identify the SQL statements that have improved, remained unchanged, or regressed after the system change.
- Tune any regressed SQL statements that are identified.

The DBMS_SQLPA package contains procedures and functions specific to the SQL Performance Analyzer. These are used to create and execute analyses and report on their findings:

- **CREATE_ANALYSIS_TASK** -- You can use different forms of this function to create analysis tasks for: a single SQL statement from various sources (the SQL text, the AWR, or the cursor cache) or for a SQL tuning set.
- **EXECUTE_ANALYSIS_TASK** -- This function and procedure executes a previously created analysis task, the function version returning the new execution name.
- **REPORT_ANALYSIS_TASK** -- This procedure displays the results of an analysis task.

## Database Replay

Oracle Database Replay captures all external database calls made to the system during the workload capture period. The capture includes all relevant information about the client request, such as SQL text, bind values, and transaction information. Background activities of the database and scheduler jobs are not captured. In addition, the following types of client requests are not captured in a workload:

- Direct path load of data from external files using utilities such as SQL*Loader
- Shared server requests (Oracle MTS)
- Oracle Streams
- Advanced replication streams
- Non-PL/SQL based Advanced Queuing (AQ)
- Flashback queries
- Oracle Call Interface (OCI) based object navigations
- Non SQL-based object access
- Distributed transactions

It is a best practice to restart the database before capturing the production workload. This ensures that ongoing and dependent transactions are allowed to be completed or rolled back before the capture begins. If the database is not restarted before the capture, transactions that are in progress or have yet to be committed will be only partially captured in the workload.

By default, all activities from all user sessions are recorded during workload capture. Workload filters can be used to include or exclude specific user sessions during the workload capture. You can use either inclusion filters or exclusion filters in a workload capture, but not both simultaneously. Inclusion filters specify user sessions that will be captured in the workload. Exclusion filters enable you to specify user sessions that will not be captured in the workload. To add filters to a workload capture, you use the DBMS_WORKLOAD_CAPTURE.ADD_FILTER procedure. To

remove an existing filter, you use the
DBMS_WORKLOAD_CAPTURE.DELETE_FILTER procedure.

You should have a well-defined starting point for the workload so that the
database being used to replay the workload can be restored to the same
point before starting the captured workload. It is best not to have any
active user sessions when starting a workload capture. Active sessions
may have ongoing transactions which will not be replayed completely.
Consider restarting the database in RESTRICTED mode prior to starting the
workload capture. When the workload capture begins, the database will
automatically switch to UNRESTRICTED mode and normal operations can
continue while the workload is being captured. You begin a workload
capture using the procedure
DBMS_WORKLOAD_CAPTURE.START_CAPTURE. To stop a workload
capture in progress, you use the
DBMS_WORKLOAD_CAPTURE.FINISH_CAPTURE procedure.

You can export AWR data from the production machine in order to enable
detailed analysis of the workload on both systems. This data is required if
you plan to run the AWR Compare Period report on a pair of workload
captures or replays. To export AWR data, you use the
DBMS_WORKLOAD_CAPTURE.EXPORT_AWR procedure.

The following views allow you to monitor a workload capture. You can
also use Oracle Enterprise Manager to monitor a workload capture:

- **DBA_WORKLOAD_CAPTURES** -- Lists all the workload captures
  that have been created in the current database.
- **DBA_WORKLOAD_FILTERS** -- Lists all workload filters used for
  workload captures defined in the current database.

After the workload has been captured, it's necessary to preprocess the
capture files prior to using them in a replay. Preprocessing converts the
captured data into replay files and creates the required metadata needed
to replay the workload. After preprocessing the captured workload, it can
be replayed multiple times on any replay system running the same

version of Oracle. As a general rule, it's recommended to move the capture files to another system for preprocessing. While the capture itself has a minimal overhead, workload preprocessing can be time consuming and resource intensive. It is better that this step be performed on the test system where the workload will be replayed rather than on the production database. Capture files are processed using the DBMS_WORKLOAD_REPLAY.PROCESS_CAPTURE procedure.

After you have preprocessed a captured workload, it can be replayed on the test system. In the workload replay, Oracle will perform the actions recorded during the workload capture. It will re-create all captured external client requests with the same timing, concurrency, and transaction dependencies that occurred on the production system. Database Replay uses a program called the replay client to re-create the external client requests. You may need to use multiple replay clients depending on the scope of the captured workload. The replay client has an imbedded calibration tool to help determine the number of replay clients required for a given workload. The entire workload from the production database is replayed. This includes DML and SQL queries, so the data in the replay system must be as logically similar to the data in the capture system as possible.

## Use Resource Manager to manage resources

The Oracle Database Resource Manager (DRM) is designed to optimize resource allocation among concurrent database sessions. It attempts to prevent problems that can happen if the operating system makes resource decisions when presented with high overhead without having awareness of the database needs. DRM helps to overcome these problems by giving the database more control over how hardware resources are allocated. DRM enables you to classify sessions into groups based on session attributes, and then allocate resources to those groups in a way that optimizes hardware utilization for your application environment. The information that performs the functions of classifying sessions and assigning resources is called a resource plan. Oracle 12c comes with several predefined resource plans that provide resource management directives that should provide immediate benefits for the majority of database installations:

- **DEFAULT_MAINTENANCE_PLAN** -- Default plan for maintenance windows.
- **DEFAULT_PLAN** -- Basic default plan that prioritizes SYS_GROUP operations and allocates minimal resources for automated maintenance and diagnostics operations.
- **DSS_PLAN** -- Example plan for a data warehouse that prioritizes critical DSS queries over non-critical DSS queries and ETL operations.
- **ETL_CRITICAL_PLAN** -- Example plan for a data warehouse that prioritizes ETL operations over DSS queries.
- **INTERNAL_QUIESCE** -- For quiescing the database. This plan cannot be activated directly. To activate, use the QUIESCE command.
- **MIXED_WORKLOAD_PLAN** -- Example plan for a mixed workload that prioritizes interactive operations over batch operations.

There are three elements of DRM:

- **Resource consumer group**: A group of sessions that are grouped together based on resource requirements.
- **Resource plan**: A container for directives that specify how resources are allocated to resource consumer groups.
- **Resource plan directive**: Associates a resource consumer group with a particular plan and specifies how resources are to be allocated to that resource consumer group.

## Resource Plan Directives

A resource plan directive for a consumer group, can specify limits for CPU and I/O resource consumption for sessions in that group. This is done by specifying the action to be taken if a call within a session exceeds one of the specified limits. These actions, called switches, occur only for sessions that are running and consuming resources, not waiting for user input or for CPU cycles. The possible actions are the following:

- The session is switched to a consumer group with lower resource allocations.
- The session is killed (terminated).
- The session's current SQL statement is aborted.

The resource plan directive attribute that determines which of the above three actions will be taken is SWITCH_GROUP. This attribute specifies the consumer group to which a session is switched if the specified criteria are met. If the value of this parameter is a consumer group, the session will be switched to that group. If the group name is 'CANCEL_SQL', the current call for that session is canceled. Finally, if the group name is 'KILL_SESSION', then the session is killed.

**Per session I/O or CPU Limits**

The resource plan directive attributes that can be used in specifying the criteria to use in making switch determinations follow. If not set, all default to UNLIMITED.

- **SWITCH_TIME**: Specifies the time (in CPU seconds) that a call can execute before an action is taken.
- **SWITCH_IO_MEGABYTES**: Specifies the number of megabytes of I/O that a session can transfer (read and write) before being switched.
- **SWITCH_IO_REQS**: Specifies the number of I/O requests that a session can execute before an action is taken.

There are two resource plan attributes that can be used to modify the behavior of resource plan switching:

- **SWITCH_ESTIMATE**: If TRUE, the database estimates the execution time of each call. If the estimated execution time exceeds SWITCH_TIME, the session is moved to the SWITCH_GROUP before beginning the call. The default is FALSE.
- **SWITCH_FOR_CALL**: If TRUE, a session that was automatically switched to another consumer group is returned to its original consumer group when the top level call completes. The default is NULL.

## Implement Application Tuning

My next trick after describing how to implement application tuning for an Oracle database in a single chapter will be to write out instructions on how to achieve world peace using a cocktail napkin and a crayon.

The techniques for tuning an Oracle database fill books – really big books. The potential questions that OU might ask a question on regarding a topic this broad are staggering. For that reason, the best I can do in this chapter is to provide advice painted in very broad strokes.

- **Tune for a Reason** – Too many database administrators tune for the wrong reason – e.g. "It's Tuesday. Tuesday starts with 'TU' so I should tune the database." Until a performance problem has been identified in a database, tuning is not a solution. That is not to say that a database administrator cannot proactively search for red flags. If you locate a SQL statement that is consuming a significant amount of CPU, that is a potential performance problem. Working to tune that statement is a legitimate task for a DBA.
- **Gather Data** – Before changing anything, you should use the tools provided with Oracle to gather information about the performance problem. Making changes in the absence of data is often a waste of time. The past several releases of the Oracle Database have added a significant suite of utilities that are specifically designed to gather data on the most common causes of performance issues. Make use of them before taking any action.

- **Make Discrete Changes** – When the time comes to start making changes, make them one at a time and then test. When multiple changes are implemented simultaneously, it is impossible to tell which change (if any) has helped the problem. Likewise, if performance gets worse, it is impossible to identify which change hurt. This is especially important if you are making changes that can affect behavior system-wide. A change that improves performance during the ten-minutes that you are testing might well cause other problems after testing has completed.
- **Stop** – Once you have implemented a fix for the identified performance issue, do not continue tuning. Even though you have started tuning, do not bypass rule one and continue tuning in the absence of a problem just because you are on a roll.
- **Monitor** – As a good DBA, obviously you monitor the performance of your database daily. However, for the next several days, pay extra attention to any elements of the database that might have been affected by the changes that were made. The bigger and broader the change that was made, the longer you should continue to monitor the database for unintended consequences.

# Storage

## Manage database structures

Oracle Enterprise Manager Express (EM Express) has the ability to perform a number of basic administrative capabilities. From the web interface, you can view, create, and alter the various storage structures of the database. When you first log into EM Express, you will be presented with a page similar to the below:

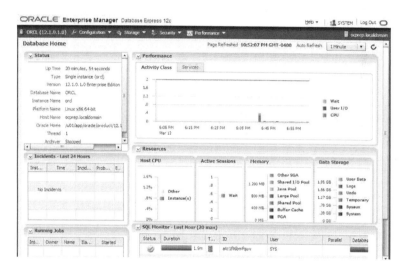

At the top of the screen, the second option from the left is 'Storage'. Clicking this will open a drop-down menu of the various storage structure types in an Oracle database. Selecting an option will open one of the following screens.

## Tablespaces

This screen allows you to perform standard administrative options related to tablespaces, including creating, dropping, adding datafiles, changing the status (i.e. to read-only), and more.

## Undo Management

This primary purpose of this screen is to display statistics about the undo tablespace. There is seldom a need for a second undo tablespace and the one tablespace requires little management. This screen is primarily useful in verifying that your undo tablespace is sized correctly for the activity in your database.

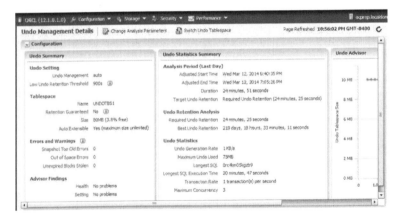

## Redo Log Groups

As with the tablespaces screen, this page allows you to perform multiple administrative functions on the redo log groups: creating, dropping, adding members, and so on. You can easily see which log group is current, if a group has been archived, and more.

## Archive Logs

This screen allows you to view information about archive logs.

## Control Files:

This screen shows a significant amount of information regarding the control files in your database. The only administrative function is the ability to backup the control file to trace.

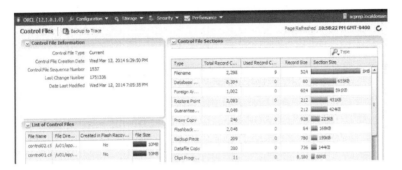

## Oracle Managed Files

The Oracle Managed Files (OMF) feature of Oracle is intended to simplify the administration of the files associated with an Oracle database. When using OMF, the administrator specifies file system directories for various file types. The database will then automatically creates, name, and manage files at the database object level in those locations. When creating a tablespace, for example, the name and path of the data file does not need to be specified with the DATAFILE clause. OMF works well with a logical volume manager (LVM), but it cannot be used with raw devices. OMF can be used to create and delete files as needed for the following database structures:

- Tablespaces
- Redo log files
- Control files
- Archived logs
- Block change tracking files
- Flashback logs
- RMAN backups

OMF is not involved with the creation or naming of administrative files such as tracefiles, audit files, alert logs, and core files.

There are three initialization parameters used to specify the file system directory to be used for the type of file. The file system directories specified must already exist. OMF will not create them. The directories must also have the OS-level permissions to allow the database to create files. When OMF is used, Oracle will ensures that a unique file is created and that it is deleted when no longer needed. The following initialization parameters are used for OMF:

- **DB_CREATE_FILE_DEST** -- Defines the default location where the database creates data files or temp files. This is also used as the default location for redo log and control files if DB_CREATE_ONLINE_LOG_DEST_n is not specified.
- **DB_CREATE_ONLINE_LOG_DEST_n** -- Defines the default location for redo log files and control file creation. By changing n, you can use this initialization parameter multiple times, where n specifies a multiplexed copy of the redo log or control file. You can specify up to five multiplexed copies.
- **DB_RECOVERY_FILE_DEST** -- Defines the location of the Fast Recovery Area. It will be used as the default location for redo log and control files or multiplexed copies of redo log and control files if DB_CREATE_ONLINE_LOG_DEST_n is not specified.

## Administer ASM

Oracle Automatic Storage Management (ASM) is a storage solution for Oracle Database files. It acts as a volume manager to provide a file system for the exclusive use of the database. When using ASM, partitioned disks are assigned to ASM with specifications for striping and mirroring. When making use of Automatic Storage Management, in addition to any database instances that exist, there will be an instance dedicated to ASM. Oracle ASM also makes use of the Oracle Managed Files (OMF) feature. OMF automatically creates files in the locations designated, as well as naming them. It also removes the files automatically when tablespaces or files are deleted from within Oracle. The ASM instance exists to manage the disk space and distribute the I/O load across multiple drives to optimize performance. ASM provides several benefits over using standard data files:

- Simplifies operations such as creating databases and managing disk space
- Distributes data across physical disks to provide uniform performance
- Rebalances data automatically after storage configuration changes

An Oracle ASM instance uses the same basic technology as an Oracle Database instance. The System Global Area (SGA) and background processes of an ASM instance are similar to those of Oracle Database. The SGA for an ASM instance is much smaller than a database instance and has fewer internal components because the ASM instance has fewer functions. The only function of an ASM instance is to mount disk groups and make the associated file available to database instances. There is no database instance mounted by Oracle ASM instances. The logical storage elements of an Oracle ASM instance are:

- **ASM Disks** -- A storage device that is provisioned to an Oracle ASM disk group. It can be a physical disk or partition, a Logical Unit Number (LUN) from a storage array, a logical volume, or a network-attached file.
- **ASM Disk Groups** -- A collection of Oracle ASM disks managed as a logical unit.
- **ASM Files** -- A file stored in an Oracle ASM disk group. The database can store data files, control files, online redo log files, and other types of files as Oracle ASM files.
- **ASM Extents** -- The raw storage used to hold the contents of an Oracle ASM file. An ASM file consists of one or more file extents and an ASM extent consists of one or more ASM allocation units.
- **ASM Allocation Units** -- The fundamental unit of allocation within a disk group.

- **ASM Instances** -- A special Oracle instance that manages Oracle ASM disks. They manage the metadata of the disk group and provide file layout information to the database instances.

Oracle ASM supports the majority of file types required by the database. The list below shows the most commonly used file types and default template that provides the attributes for file creation. Oracle ASM cannot directly support some administrative file types on disk groups. These include trace files, audit files, alert logs, export files, and core files.

- **Control files** -- CONTROLFILE
- **Data files** -- DATAFILE
- **Redo log files** -- ONLINELOG
- **Archive log files** -- ARCHIVELOG
- **Temporary files** -- TEMPFILE
- **Data file backup pieces** -- BACKUPSET
- **Archive log backup piece** -- BACKUPSET
- **Persistent initialization parameter file (SPFILE)** -- PARAMETERFILE
- **Flashback logs** -- FLASHBACK
- **Data Pump dumpset** -- DUMPSET

**Fully Qualified File Name Form**

Whenever a file is created in ASM, Oracle Managed Files automatically generates a fully qualified file name for it. The fully qualified filename represents a complete path name in the Oracle ASM file system. You can use a fully qualified file name for referencing existing Oracle ASM files in Oracle ASM operations, except for disk group creation. A fully qualified file name has the following form:

**+diskgroup/dbname/filetype/filetypetag.file.incarnation.**

The definitions of the individual elements are:

- **+diskgroup** -- The disk group name preceded by a plus sign. The plus sign (+) is equivalent to the root directory for the Oracle ASM file system.
- **dbname** -- The DB_UNIQUE_NAME of the database to which the file belongs.
- **filetype** -- The Oracle file type and can be one of the file types shown in Table 7–3.
- **filetypetag** -- Type-specific information about the file.
- **file.incarnation** -- The file/incarnation pair, used to ensure uniqueness.

An example of a fully qualified Oracle ASM filename is:

**+data/ocpdb/controlfile/Current.221.46544321**

The file creation request does not specify the fully qualified filename. It supplies an alias or just a disk group name. Oracle ASM then creates the file in the correct Oracle ASM path based on the file type. ASM then assigns an appropriate fully qualified filename. If an alias is specified in the creation request, ASM creates the alias and points it to the fully qualified filename. ASM file creation requests are either single or multiple file creation requests.

### Alias Filenames

Alias filenames can be used for referencing existing files and creating new ASM files. Alias names consist of the disk group name preceded by a plus sign followed by a name string. Alias filenames use a hierarchical directory structure, with the slash (/) or backslash (\) character separating name components. Aliases must include the disk group name. They cannot exist at the root level (+). When a file is created with an alias, both the alias and fully-qualified names are recorded and you can access the file with either name. Alias filenames do not (and cannot) end in a dotted pair of numbers. Examples of alias filenames include:

- +data/ocpdb/control_file_main
- +data/ocpdb/control_file_bkup
- +fra/recover/second.dbf

The example below creates an undo tablespace with a data file that has an alias name, and with attributes that are set by the user-defined template my_undo_template. This example assumes that the **ocpdb** directory has been created in disk group **data**.

```
CREATE UNDO TABLESPACE ocpundo
DATAFILE '+data/ocpdb/ocp_undo_ts' SIZE 200M;
```

If an alias is used to create the data file, it is not an Oracle Managed Files (OMF) file. This means that the file will not be automatically deleted when the tablespace is dropped. To drop the file manually after the tablespace has been dropped, use the following SQL statement:

```
ALTER DISKGROUP data DROP FILE '+data/ocpdb/ocp_undo_ts';
```

## Manage ASM disks and diskgroups

An ASM disk group consists of multiple disks and is the fundamental object that Oracle ASM manages. Disk groups contain the information required to manage drive space. The sub-components of disk groups include disks, files, and allocation units. A given file is contained within a single disk group. However, a disk group can contain files from several databases. A single database can use files from multiple disk groups.

## Disk Group Attributes

Disk group attributes are parameters that are bound to a disk group rather than an Oracle ASM instance. Some of the more common attributes are below. Refer to the Oracle ASM Administrator's Guide for more details.

- **ACCESS_CONTROL.ENABLED** -- This attribute determines whether Oracle ASM File Access Control is enabled for a disk group. The value can be true or false. The default is false. This attribute can only be set when altering a disk group.
- **ACCESS_CONTROL.UMASK** -- This attribute determines which permissions are masked out on the creation of an Oracle ASM file for the user that owns the file, users in the same user group, and others not in the user group. This attribute applies to all files on a disk group.
- **AU_SIZE** -- A file extent consists of one or more allocation units. An Oracle ASM file consists of one or more file extents. When you create a disk group, you can set the Oracle ASM allocation unit size with the AU_SIZE disk group attribute. The values can be 1, 2, 4, 8, 16, 32, or 64 MB, depending on the specific disk group compatibility level.
- **COMPATIBLE.ASM** -- This attribute controls the format of data structures for ASM metadata in the given disk group. The ASM software version must be equal or greater than this value in order to be able to access the disk group. The COMPATIBLE.ASM attribute must always be greater than or equal to COMPATIBLE.RDBMS for the same disk group. For example, you can set COMPATIBLE.ASM for the disk group to 11.0 and COMPATIBLE.RDBMS for the disk group to 10.1. In this case, the disk group can be managed only by ASM software with a version of 11.0 or higher. However, any database client of version 10.1 or higher can use the disk group. If you will be increasing both parameters, the COMPATIBLE.ASM value must be increased first.
- **COMPATIBLE.RDBMS** -- This dictates the format of messages that are exchanged between the Automatic Storage Management instance and the database instance. This parameter set the minimum database client release that may access a given disk group. You can set different values of this parameter on

diskgroups within the same ASM instance for multiple database clients running at different compatibility settings.

- **CONTENT.TYPE** -- Identifies the disk group type: data, recovery, or system. The type value determines the distance to the nearest neighbor disk in the failure group where Oracle ASM mirrors copies of the data. The default value is 'data' which specifies a distance of 1 to the nearest neighbor disk. A value of 'recovery' specifies a distance of 3 to the nearest neighbor disk and a value of 'system' specifies a distance of 5.

- **DISK_REPAIR_TIME** -- Determines the amount of time that a disk can be unavailable due to a transient failure before to being dropped permanently from the diskgroup. To use this parameter, both the compatible.rdbms and compatible.asm attributes must be set to at least 11.1. You cannot set this attribute when creating a disk group, but you can alter the DISK_REPAIR_TIME attribute in an ALTER DISKGROUP ... SET ATTRIBUTE statement to change the default value. If both compatible.rdbms and compatible.asm are set to at least 11.1, then the default is 3.6 hours. If either parameter is less than 11.1, the disk is dropped immediately if it becomes inaccessible. The time can be specified in units of minutes by using the letter M or hours by using the letter H. If you provide a number with no unit, then the default is hours. The default attribute value can be changed while bringing the disk offline by using an ALTER DISKGROUP ... DISK OFFLINE statement and the DROP AFTER clause. If a disk is taken offline using the current value of DISK_REPAIR_TIME, and the value of this attribute for the diskgroup is subsequently changed with the ALTER DISKGROUP ... SET ATTRIBUTE statement, then the changed value is used by ASM in determining when to drop the disk.

## CREATE DISKGROUP

The CREATE DISKGROUP SQL statement is used to create disk groups. When creating a disk group, you specify the following information:

- A unique name to the disk group.
- The redundancy level of the disk group. For Oracle ASM to mirror files, specify the redundancy level as NORMAL REDUNDANCY (2-

way mirroring by default for most file types) or HIGH
REDUNDANCY (3-way mirroring for all files). Specify EXTERNAL
REDUNDANCY if you do not want mirroring by Oracle ASM.

- The disks that are to be formatted as Oracle ASM disks belonging
  to the disk group.
- Optionally specify the disks as belonging to specific failure groups.
- Optionally specify the type of failure group.
- Optionally specify disk group attributes, such as software
  compatibility or allocation unit size.

The SQL statement below creates a disk group named data with normal
redundancy. It consists of two failure groups: fg1 or fg2 with three disks in
each failure group. The data disk group is typically used to store database
data files.

```
CREATE DISKGROUP data NORMAL REDUNDANCY
FAILGROUP fg1 DISK
'/devices/diska1' NAME diska1,
'/devices/diska2' NAME diska2,
'/devices/diska3' NAME diska3
FAILGROUP fg2 DISK
'/devices/diskb1' NAME diskb1,
'/devices/diskb2' NAME diskb2,
'/devices/diskb3' NAME diskb3
ATTRIBUTE 'au_size'='2M',
'compatible.asm' = '11.2',
'compatible.rdbms' = '11.2';
```

## ALTER DISKGROUP

The ALTER DISKGROUP SQL statement enables you to alter a disk group
configuration. It is possible to add, resize, or drop disks while the
database remains online. Multiple operations in a single ALTER
DISKGROUP statement are both possible and recommended. Grouping
operations in a single ALTER DISKGROUP statement can reduce
rebalancing operations. Oracle ASM automatically rebalances a disk group
when its configuration changes. The V$ASM_OPERATION view allows you
to monitor the status of rebalance operations. The following command
adds two more disks to the data diskgroup.

```
ALTER DISKGROUP data ADD DISK
'/devices/diska4' NAME diska4,
'/devices/diska5' NAME diska5;
```

When rebalancing a disk group, if the POWER clause is not specified in an ALTER DISKGROUP statement, or if a rebalance is executed implicitly because a disk has been added or dropped, the ASM_POWER_LIMIT initialization parameter determines the power used. The value of this parameter can be adjusted dynamically. Higher power values will cause a rebalance operation to complete faster, but consumes more processing and I/O resources. The default value of 1 minimizes disruption to other applications.

## Manage ASM instance

An Oracle ASM instance is started much like an Oracle database instance with some minor differences. When starting an Oracle ASM instance, note the following:

You must set the ORACLE_SID environment variable to the Oracle ASM system identifier (SID). The default Oracle ASM SID for a single-instance database is +ASM, and the default SID for Oracle ASM for an Oracle RAC node is +ASMnode_number where node_number is the number of the node. The ORACLE_HOME environment variable must be set to the Grid Infrastructure home where Oracle ASM was installed.

- The initialization parameter file must contain the following entry: INSTANCE_TYPE = ASM. This indicates that it is an Oracle ASM instance rather than a database instance.
- When you run the STARTUP command, rather than trying to mount and open a database, this command attempts to mount Oracle ASM disk groups.

An ASM instance interprets SQL*Plus STARTUP command parameters differently than a database instance.

- **FORCE** -- Issues a SHUTDOWN ABORT to the Oracle ASM instance before restarting it.
- **MOUNT or OPEN** -- Mounts the disk groups specified in the ASM_DISKGROUPS initialization parameter. This is the default. An OPEN state for an ASM instance doesn't really exist. If supplied, this parameter is simply treated as MOUNT.
- **NOMOUNT** -- Starts up the Oracle ASM instance without mounting any disk groups.
- **RESTRICT** -- Starts up an instance in restricted mode. Only users with both the CREATE SESSION and RESTRICTED SESSION system privileges can connect.

The SYSASM operating system privilege and the OSASM operating system group allow storage responsibilities to be assigned to System Administrators without granting high-level access to the Oracle database itself. Users can be created in the ASM instance and granted the SYSASM privilege. This allows them to connect to the ASM instance and perform administration tasks. Similarly, assigning an operating system user to the OSASM group would allow then to connect as SYSASM using OS authentication.

```
$ export ORACLE_SID=+ASM
$ sqlplus / as sysasm

CREATE USER asm_admin IDENTIFIED by badpassword_nobiscuit;
User created.

SQL> GRANT SYSASM TO asm_admin;


SQLPLUS /NOLOG
SQL> CONNECT asm_admin AS SYSASM
Enter password: badpassword_nobiscuit
Connected to an idle instance.
```

```
SQL> STARTUP
ASM instance started
Total System Global Area 71303168 bytes
Fixed Size 1069292 bytes
Variable Size 45068052 bytes
ASM Cache 25165824 bytes
ASM disk groups mounted
```

## Shutting Down an Oracle ASM Instance

An ASM instance is shut down using the SHUTDOWN command in SQL*Plus just as with a database instance. As with startup, you must ensure that the ORACLE_SID environment variable is set to the Oracle ASM SID before connecting to SQL*Plus. Before you shut down an ASM instance, you should shut down all database instances that use it. You should also dismount all file systems mounted on Oracle ASM Dynamic Volume Manager volumes before attempting to shut down the ASM instance.

To shut down an Oracle ASM instance, perform the following steps:

```
SQLPLUS /NOLOG
SQL> CONNECT asm_admin AS SYSASM
Enter password: badpassword_nobiscuit
Connected.
SQL> SHUTDOWN NORMAL
```

The SHUTDOWN modes when used with an Oracle ASM instance are:

- **NORMAL** -- The instance waits for any in-progress SQL to complete before dismounting all of the disk groups and shutting down. The instance also waits for all currently connected users to disconnect from the instance. If any database instances are connected to the ASM instance, then the SHUTDOWN command aborts and returns an error. NORMAL is the default mode.
- **IMMEDIATE or TRANSACTIONAL** -- The instance waits for any in-progress SQL to complete before dismounting all of the disk groups and shutting down the Oracle ASM instance. It does not wait for users currently connected to the instance to disconnect. If any database instances are connected to the Oracle ASM

235

instance, then the SHUTDOWN aborts with an error. ASM instances have no transactions, so TRANSACTIONAL and IMMEDIATE are equivalent.

- **ABORT** -- The instance immediately shuts down without the orderly dismount of disk groups. This requires recovery on the next Oracle ASM startup. Any database instances that are connected to the Oracle ASM instance will also perform a shutdown abort because their storage will no longer be available.

## Manage VLDB

Storage in a Very Large Database is almost always managed through the use of partitioning. Partitioning improves Oracle's ability to support very large tables by breaking them into smaller and more manageable pieces called partitions. Partitioned tables facilitate SQL tuning by allowing SQL statements to avoid scanning partitions that can be determined not to hold the required data using partition pruning. Partitioning can also facilitate SQL tuning by breaking down large joins of similarly-partitioned objects by using partition-wise joins. Partitioning of tables and indexes works hand-in-hand with parallel queries to improve performance in data warehouses. When an object in the database is partitioned, it is possible for parallel server processes to scan individual table partitions or index partitions when doing so makes sense.

### Partitioning Methods

There are three fundamental methods used to control how data is distributed into partitions: Range, Hash, and List. When partitioning data using these methods, it is possible to partition a table at a single-level, or to partition it at two levels for composite partitioning. There are advantages and design considerations for both methods. The specific needs of a given table determine which strategy is more appropriate.

**Single-Level Partitioning**

In single-level partitioning, a table is defined by specifying one of the following three methodologies, where one or more columns in the table act as the partitioning key:

- **Range Partitioning** -- This method maps data to partitions based on ranges of values of the partitioning key. Each of the partitions is defined with a range of values that determines which records should be placed in it. This is the most common type of partitioning and is often used with dates. Partitions are created with a VALUES LESS THAN clause, which specifies a non-inclusive upper bound for the partitions. Rows that have partitioning key values equal to or higher than this literal are added to the next higher partition. The lower bound is implied by the VALUES LESS THAN clause of the previous partition. The first partition has no lower bound. The highest partition can use a MAXVALUE literal. This represents a virtual infinite value that sorts higher than any other possible value for the partitioning key, including NULL.

- **Hash Partitioning** -- This method uses a hashing algorithm to map data to partitions using the partitioning key that you identify. The hashing algorithm is designed to evenly distribute rows among each of the partitions. This is an ideal method to distribute data evenly across devices. It is easier to implement than range partitioning. Hash partitioning is especially useful when the data to be partitioned is not historical or has no obvious partitioning key.

- **List Partitioning** -- This method allows you to specify a list of discrete values for the partitioning key in the description for each partition. In this fashion, you can control exactly how rows map to partitions. List partitioning provides the ability to group unordered and unrelated sets of data. In list partitioning, the DEFAULT partition provides a partition to store all values that are not explicitly mapped to any other partition.

**Composite Partitioning**

This strategy combines the basic data distribution methods. In composite partitioning, a table is partitioned by one data distribution method and then each partition is further subdivided into subpartitions using a second data distribution method. It is possible for the partitioning methods at the two levels to be the same, or different. Composite partitioning provides higher degrees of potential partition pruning and finer granularity of data placement. The possible composite partitioning methods are:

- Range-Range Partitioning
- Range-Hash Partitioning
- Range-List Partitioning
- List-Range Partitioning
- List-Hash Partitioning
- List-List Partitioning

# Implement Space Management

One of the first (and easiest) steps to manage space effectively in tablespaces is to ensure that all tablespaces are locally managed. A tablespace that is locally managed uses bitmaps within the tablespace itself to track all extent information. Local management has several benefits over traditional tablespaces where this information is stored in the data dictionary:

- Space allocations and deallocations modify locally managed resources. This makes them fast and concurrent, resulting in enhanced performance.
- Locally managed temporary tablespaces do not generate any undo or redo.
- If the AUTOALLOCATE clause is specified, the database automatically selects the appropriate extent size.
- Reliance on the data dictionary is reduced, reducing contention in times of high activity to tables.
- There is no need to coalesce free extents.

Any tablespace can be locally managed, including SYSTEM and SYSAUX. There are maintenance procedures in the DBMS_SPACE_ADMIN package specific to locally managed tablespaces.

The syntax to create a locally managed tablespace, is the keyword LOCAL in the EXTENT MANAGEMENT clause of the CREATE TABLESPACE statement. The default value for new permanent tablespaces is 'EXTENT MANAGEMENT LOCAL AUTOALLOCATE'. Specifying this clause is optional unless you do not want local management or you want to use the UNIFORM keyword rather than AUTOALLOCATE. When the AUTOALLOCATE keyword is used, the database will manage extents automatically. If you want the tablespace to utilize uniform extents of a specific size, you must specify the UNIFORM keyword. The two commands below will have identical effects:

```
CREATE TABLESPACE ocpts
DATAFILE '/u02/oracle/data/ocpts01.dbf' SIZE 50M
EXTENT MANAGEMENT LOCAL AUTOALLOCATE;

CREATE TABLESPACE ocpts
DATAFILE '/u02/oracle/data/ocpts01.dbf' SIZE 50M;
```

There are two methods that Oracle Database can use to manage segment space in a locally managed tablespace. Manual space management uses freelists to manage free space in a segment. Automatic segment space management uses bitmaps. Automatic segment space management is more efficient method, and is the default for all new permanent, locally managed tablespaces. You can explicitly enable it with the SEGMENT SPACE MANAGEMENT AUTO clause:

```
CREATE TABLESPACE ocpts
DATAFILE '/u02/oracle/data/ocpts01.dbf' SIZE 50M
EXTENT MANAGEMENT LOCAL AUTOALLOCATE
SEGMENT SPACE MANAGEMENT AUTO;
```

## Basic Table Compression

Basic Table Compression is the most limited of the available compression methods. Basic Compression does not apply compression to DML operations (INSERT/UPDATE) performed on a table. Data is only compressed when it is loaded into a table via bulk load operations. It is included with Oracle Database Enterprise Edition (EE). The compressed formats on disk for Basic Compression and Advanced Row Compression are identical, so it is technically possible to convert from Basic to Advanced Compression simply by changing the storage definition on the table or partition.

## Advanced Row Compression

Advanced Row Compression was originally called OLTP Table compression when it was released in Oracle Database 11g. It compresses data for all types of data manipulation operations, including conventional DML such as INSERT and UPDATE. Advanced Row Compression also minimizes the overhead of write operations on compressed data. Advanced Row Compression is a part of the Advanced Compression option. The algorithm for Advanced Row Compression works by eliminating duplicate values within a database block, even across multiple columns.

## Hybrid Columnar Compression

Hybrid Columnar Compression (HCC) technology is a method for organizing data within a set of database blocks. In order to use HCC, the underlying file system must support it. HCC requires the use of Oracle Storage – Exadata, Pillar Axiom or Sun ZFS Storage Appliance. It stored data in a combination of both row and columnar methods. HCC-compressed data is stored in logical construct referred to as a compression unit. When data is loaded into a table using HCC, groups of rows are stored in columnar format, with the values for a column stored and compressed together. The column data for a set of rows is then compressed and placed into the compression unit. Because the data from a given has the same data type and similar characteristics, the compression algorithm is more effective. HCC compression ratios typically range from 6x to 15x depending the on the type used.

Tables created in a tablespace with the compression option enabled will default to that method. However, you can create tables uncompressed or using a different method by supplying a compression clause in the CREATE TABLE statement. If you alter the default compression in a tablespace, all new tables created will default to the new method, but existing tables are unchanged.

## Segment Shrink

The online segment shrink capability of Oracle allows you to reclaim fragmented free space below the high watermark in a segment. Shrinking a segment provides the following benefits:

- Compaction of data leads to better cache utilization.
- Compacted data requires fewer blocks to be scanned in full table scans.

Segment shrink is an online, in-place operation that does not interfere with DML operations or queries. Concurrent DML operations are blocked for a short time at the end of the shrink operation, when the space is deallocated. Indexes are maintained during the shrink operation and remain usable after completion. No extra disk space needs to be allocated. Segment shrink reclaims unused space both above and below the high water mark. By default, a shrink operation compacts the segment, adjusts the high water mark, and releases the reclaimed space.

Segment shrink requires that rows be moved to new locations. You must first enable row movement in the object and disable any rowid-based triggers. Shrink operations can be performed only on segments in locally managed tablespaces with automatic segment space management (ASSM). Within an ASSM tablespace, all segment types are eligible for online segment shrink except the following:

- IOT mapping tables
- Tables with rowid based materialized views
- Tables with function-based indexes
- SECUREFILE LOBs
- Compressed tables

**Invoking Online Segment Shrink**

You can shrink space in a table, index-organized table, index, partition, subpartition, materialized view, or materialized view log. You do this using ALTER TABLE, ALTER INDEX, ALTER MATERIALIZED VIEW, or ALTER MATERIALIZED VIEW LOG statement with the SHRINK SPACE clause. There are two optional clauses that control the behavior of the shrink operation:

- **COMPACT** – This clause divides the shrink segment operation into two phases. When specified, the Database defragments the segment space and compacts the table rows but does not reset the high water mark or deallocate space. You can reissue the SHRINK SPACE clause without the COMPACT clause during off-peak hours to complete the shrink operation.
- **CASCADE** – This clause extends the segment shrink operation to all dependent segments of the object.

## Examples

## Shrink a table and all of its dependent segments:

```
ALTER TABLE employees
SHRINK SPACE CASCADE;
```

## Shrink a single partition of a partitioned table:

```
ALTER TABLE customers
MODIFY PARTITION cust_P1 SHRINK SPACE;
```

# Security

## Develop and implement a security policy

The security policy for a database establishes methods for protecting it from accidental or malicious damage. The Oracle database has excellent protections to protect against data loss due to hardware and other failures. Protecting the data against internal failures caused by legitimate database users, or by individuals who have managed to access the database illegitimately (for example by obtaining the credentials of a legitimate user) is the task of the database administrator. Well-created security policies can:

- Reduce the possibility of an attacker gaining access to the database.
- Minimize the damage that can be caused from user-level accounts.
- Detect attempts to illicitly gain access to the database or restricted data.

Three of primary areas requiring a defined security policy are Users, Privileges, and Auditing.

**Users**

Before anyone can connect to the database, a user must authenticate with a valid user name that has been previously defined to the database. There are a number of different ways that authentication can be set up for users in an Oracle database. The most common is by specifying a password. Since version 11g of Oracle, user account passwords are case sensitive by default. You can alter this behavior, but Oracle strongly recommends that you leave case sensitivity in passwords enabled. There are also two new password complexity verification functions with Oracle 12c: ORA12C_VERIFY_FUNCTION and ORA12C_STRONG_VERIFY_FUNCTION. Either can be used as-is or modified as desired to provide improved password security for database accounts. You can customize either function to meet your own requirements. Oracle recommends that you do so, in fact. By default, password complexity verification is not enabled. Enabling either of these functions can significantly reduce the possibility of attackers gaining access to your database.

## Privileges and Roles

Once a user has been authenticated (whether a legitimate user or an attacker), all of the database privileges that have been allocated to that user account are available. Best practice is always to assign the least amount of privileges that are required in order for them to accomplish the tasks required for their jobs. Granting unnecessary privileges to users has no positive impact and can compromise the security of the database. It is all too common for database administrators to over-grant privileges to users to ensure that they can perform a requested task (and will stop bothering them) rather than to take the time to grant only the appropriate privilege. Database users can receive a privilege in two ways:

- Explicit -- Privileges granted directly to a database user.
- Role-based -- Privileges are granted to a role. The role is then granted to one or more users.

Roles allow for much easier and better management of privileges. Ideally, you should create roles in a database that correspond to the various types of users on the database. The minimum set or required privilege can then be granted to the roles, and the roles granted to the proper users. Granting privileges in this fashion provides the optimum mix of minimizing both the privileges granted to users and the amount of work the database administrator must perform to supply those privileges to users.

**Auditing**

Auditing allows administrators (and others) to monitor and record selected user database actions, including those performed by administrators. Auditing allows you to monitor system-wide actions and actions performed on individual database objects. Oracle provides a default set of unified audit policies that contain standard audit settings. It is also possible to create custom unified audit policies. The DBMS_FGA PL/SQL package can be used to create fine-grained audit policies that are triggered by actions at a more granular level than unified auditing policies.

Auditing can help to determine if a legitimate user is attempting to exceed their level of privileges -- either to gain access to data they should not have or to maliciously damage the database. Auditing policies are also useful in detecting attempts to access the database illicitly.

## Configure and manage auditing

Oracle's auditing features monitor and record selected user database actions. Auditing is performed on actions from both database users and non-database users. Standard auditing can be based on individual actions, such as SQL statements executed or on the use of specific system or object privileges. It's possible to audit both successful and failed attempts to perform activities. Auditing must be enabled and configured for the needs of a given database. The audited actions will be recorded either in the data dictionary or in operating system files. Auditing is effective for enforcing strong internal controls. Auditing is typically used to perform the following activities:

- Enable accountability for actions.
- Deter users or intruders from inappropriate actions.
- Investigate suspicious activity.
- Notify an auditor of unauthorized actions.
- Monitor and gather data about specific database activities.

- Detect problems with an authorization or access control.
- Address auditing requirements for regulatory compliance.

Standard auditing is enabled by setting the AUDIT_TRAIL initialization parameter.

- **DB** – Directs audit records to the database audit trail, except for mandatory and SYS audit records, which are always written to the operating system audit trail. DB is the default setting for the AUDIT_TRAIL parameter.
- **DB, EXTENDED** – Same as DB, but also populates the SQL bind and SQL text CLOB-type columns of the SYS.AUD$ table with the SQL statement used in the action that was audited when available.
- **OS** – Directs all audit records to an operating system file. The AUDIT_FILE_DEST parameter determines the location of the file.
- **XML** – Writes to the operating system audit record file in XML format. The XML AUDIT_TRAIL value does not affect the syslog audit file. These records will always be in text format.
- **XML, EXTENDED** – Behaves the same as AUDIT_TRAIL=XML, but also includes SQL text and SQL bind information in the operating system XML audit files.
- **NONE** – Disables standard auditing.

The standard database audit trail is written to the SYS.AUD$ table and the fine-grained audit trail is written to SYS.FGA_LOG$. Audit records can only be deleted by someone who has connected with administrator privileges. Administrators must also be audited for unauthorized use. If the initialization parameter O7_DICTIONARY_ACCESSIBILITY is set to FALSE (the default), only SYSDBA users can perform DML on the SYS.AUD$ and SYS.FGA_LOG$ tables. Oracle Database Vault and Oracle Label Security can be used to add further protections if you have licenses for those products.

Certain database-related operations are always written to the operating system audit files. The actions of any user logged in with SYSDBA or SYSOPER are audited in this fashion. This is called mandatory auditing and will occur even if you have not enabled the database audit trail. The operating system files are in the $ORACLE_BASE/admin/$ORACLE_SID/adump directory by default.

Mandatory auditing includes the following operations:

- Database startup.
- SYSDBA and SYSOPER logins.
- Database shutdown.

Fine-grained auditing (FGA) extends the capabilities of standard auditing. FGA allows for the definition of specific conditions that will trigger an audit record. This allows for granular auditing of queries, and DML operations. Whereas standard auditing could record if a SELECT operation was performed against a table, fine-grained auditing could be set if a SELECT against a table was performed at a given time or accessed a given column or a particular set of rows. Fine Grained Auditing therefore allows for much more focused auditing with less 'noise' from false hits.

## Create the password file

The Oracle password file is required to support the administrative privileges SYSDBA, SYSOPER, SYSBACKUP, SYSDG, and SYSKM. If this file is lost or damaged, it must be recreated using the orapwd command-line utility. When a new password file is created, orapwd prompts for the SYS password and stores the result in the created password file. The syntax of the ORAPWD command is as follows:

```
ORAPWD FILE=filename [ENTRIES=numusers] [FORCE={Y|N}]
[IGNORECASE={Y|N}]
```

The command arguments of orapwd follow. For all parameters, there are no spaces permitted around the equal sign (=) character.

- **FILE** --Name to assign to the password file. You must supply a complete path. If you supply only a file name, the file is written to the current directory.
- **ENTRIES** -- Maximum number of entries (user accounts) to permit in the file. This is optional.
- **FORCE** -- If Y, permits overwriting an existing password file. This is optional.
- **IGNORECASE** -- If Y, passwords are treated as case-insensitive. This is optional.
- **FORMAT** -- When this argument is set to 12 (the default), ORAPWD creates a database password file in Oracle Database 12c format. The 12c format is required for the file to support SYSBACKUP, SYSDG, and SYSKM administrative privileges. If this argument is set to legacy, then ORAPWD creates a database password file that only supports SYSDBA and SYSOPER privileges.
- **SYSBACKUP** -- If this argument is set to y, then ORAPWD creates a SYSBACKUP entry in the password file and prompts for the password.
- **SYSDG** -- If this argument is set to y, then ORAPWD creates a SYSDG entry in the password file and prompts for the password.
- **SYSKM** -- If this argument is set to y, then ORAPWD creates a SYSKM entry in the password file and prompts for the password.

The following command creates a password file named orapworcl that allows up to 40 privileged users with different passwords.

```
orapwd FILE=orapworcl ENTRIES=40
```

The initialization parameter remote_login_passwordfile is connected to the password file. This parameter must be set to either SHARED or EXCLUSIVE. When set to SHARED, the password file can be used by multiple databases, yet only the SYS user is recognized. When set to EXCLUSIVE, the file can be used by only one database, yet multiple users can exist in the file.

The REMOTE_LOGIN_PASSWORDFILE initialization parameter is used to share or disable the password file. It can be set to one of the following values:

- **none** -- The Oracle Database will behave as if the password file does not exist.
- **exclusive** -- The password file can be used with only one database. Using an exclusive password file enables you to add, modify, and delete users. It also enables the passwords for SYS, SYSBACKUP, SYSDG, or SYSKM to be changed with the ALTER USER command. This is the default.
- **shared** -- The file can be used by multiple databases running on the same server, or multiple instances of an Oracle RAC database. A shared password file is read-only and cannot be modified. Therefore, you cannot add users to a shared password file. All users needing administrative privileges must be added to the password file when REMOTE_LOGIN_PASSWORDFILE is set to exclusive and then the value can be changed to shared.

## Implement column and tablespace encryption

Both column and tablespace encryption make use of Oracle's Transparent Data Encryption (TDE) functionality. Before making use of TDE, it is necessary to create a software keystore, which is a container that stores the TDE master encryption key. There is one keystore per database, and the database locates this keystore by checking the location defined in the sqlnet.ora file. For information on configuring a software keystore, refer to the Oracle 12c Advanced Security Guide. This chapter will assume that a keystore has been configured.

In previous releases, the Oracle software keystore was referred to as the Oracle Wallet. The Software keystore must be open before you can create an encrypted column or tablespace and before you can store or retrieve encrypted data. When you open the keystore, it is available to all sessions. It remains open until you explicitly close it or until the database is shut down.

Transparent Data Encryption is designed to protect data stored on a disk or other media. It does not offer any protection for data in transit. It protects data from unauthorized access by means other than through the database. This would include events such as someone getting hold of backup tapes of a database. TDE encryption also protects data from users who try to access database files directly through the operating system.

Oracle's TDE functionality supports industry-standard encryption algorithms, including the following: 3DES168, AES128, AES192, AES256. The encryption key length is implied by the algorithm name. For example, the AES128 algorithm uses 128-bit keys. You specify the algorithm to use when you create the encrypted column or tablespace. You can pick the algorithm to use for each tablespace or column encrypted -- they do not all have to be the same. While longer key lengths theoretically provide greater security, there is a trade-off in CPU overhead. By default, TDE uses the AES encryption algorithm with a 192-bit key length (AES192). TDE adds salt to plaintext before encrypting it in order to make it harder for attackers to steal data through a brute force attack. TDE also adds a Message Authentication Code (MAC) to the data for integrity checking. The SHA-1 integrity algorithm is used by default.

**Column Encryption**

The column encryption functionality encrypts and decrypts data at the SQL layer. Any utilities and features of Oracle that bypass the SQL layer cannot use the services provided by TDE column encryption. TDE column encryption should not be used with the following database features:

- Index types other than B-tree
- Range scan search through an index
- Synchronous change data capture
- Transportable tablespaces

It is also not possible to use TDE to encrypt columns used in foreign key constraints. If there is a need to encrypt columns using any of these unsupported features, the DBMS_CRYPTO package can be used to encrypt the data. Transparent Data Encryption (TDE).

It is possible to encrypt data columns that use the following data types: BINARY_DOUBLE, BINARY_FLOAT, CHAR, DATE, INTERVAL DAY TO SECOND, INTERVAL YEAR TO MONTH, NCHAR, NUMBER, NVARCHAR2, RAW, TIMESTAMP, VARCHAR2. The character data types have size restrictions as well. View the Advanced Security guide for more details. The following example creates a new table with an encrypted column (salary) using the default encryption algorithm (AES192).

```
CREATE TABLE employee (
emp_id        NUMBER,
first_name    VARCHAR2(128),
last_name     VARCHAR2(128),
salary        NUMBER ENCRYPT);
```

If the column being encrypted is going to be indexed, it should be encrypted without salt. The following example creates the same table as above, but encrypts the EMP_ID column with no salt, and encrypts the SALARY column using the AES256 algorithm.

```
CREATE TABLE employee (
emp_id        NUMBER  ENCRYPT NO SALT,
first_name    VARCHAR2(128),
last_name     VARCHAR2(128),
salary        NUMBER ENCRYPT USING 'AES256');
```

It is possible to add an encrypted column to an existing table with the ALTER TABLE ADD statement. The following example adds an encrypted column for the social security number to the employee table:

```
ALTER TABLE employee ADD (ssn VARCHAR2(11) ENCRYPT);
```

It is possible to encrypt an existing unencrypted column with the ALTER TABLE MODIFY statement. The following example encrypts the LAST_NAME column in the employee table.

```
ALTER TABLE employee MODIFY (last_name ENCRYPT);
```

## Tablespace Encryption

It is possible to encrypt any permanent tablespace to protect sensitive data. Tablespace encryption is transparent to database users and your applications. When a tablespace is encrypted, all tablespace blocks are encrypted. All segment types are supported for encryption, including tables, clusters, indexes, LOBs, table and index partitions, and so on. To maximize security, data from an encrypted tablespace is automatically encrypted when written to the undo tablespace, to the redo logs, and to any temporary tablespace. There is no disk space overhead for encrypting a tablespace. There are some restrictions involving encrypted tablespaces:

- You cannot encrypt an existing tablespace with an ALTER TABLESPACE statement.
- Encrypted tablespaces are subject to restrictions when transporting to another database.
- When recovering a database with encrypted tablespaces you must open the keystore that contains the encryption key after database mount and before database open, so the recovery process can decrypt data blocks and redo.

The following statement creates an encrypted tablespace with the default encryption algorithm:

```
CREATE TABLESPACE secure_ts
DATAFILE '/u02/app/oracle/oradata/orcl11g/secure01.dbf' SIZE 200M
ENCRYPTION
DEFAULT STORAGE(ENCRYPT);
```

# Performing Post-Upgrade Tasks

## Migrate to unified auditing

Unified auditing is not enabled by default for upgraded databases. The upgraded database will use the auditing functionality that was present in the earlier release. Databases that are newly created with Oracle 12c will use the mixed-mode method of unified auditing by default. Only if the migration to unified auditing is manually migrated will traditional auditing be disabled. The process to migrate to the pure unified audit facility follows:

1. Log in to SQL*Plus as user SYS with the SYSDBA privilege.

   ```
   sqlplus sys as sysdba
   ```

2. Run the following query to determine if the database has already been migrated to unified auditing. If the output is for the VALUE column is TRUE, then unified auditing is already enabled and no further steps are required.

   ```
   SELECT VALUE
   FROM   V$OPTION
   WHERE  PARAMETER = 'Unified Auditing';
   ```

3. Shut down the database.
4. Stop the listener.
5. Go to the $ORACLE_HOME /rdbms/lib directory.
6. Enable the unified auditing executable as follows:
   - For UNIX, run the following command:
     ```
     make -f ins_rdbms.mk uniaud_on ioracle
         ORACLE_HOME=$ORACLE_HOME
     ```

   - For Windows, rename the %ORACLE_HOME%/bin/orauniaud12.dll.dbl file to %ORACLE_HOME%/bin/orauniaud12.dll.
7. Restart the listener.
8. Restart the database

## Perform post-upgrade tasks

After the legacy database has been upgraded to Oracle 12c, there are a number of other tasks that should be performed. None of these steps is mandatory, but performing them is important for ensuring that you are getting the best use of the features available in 12c. The recommended tasks following an upgrade include:

- **Back Up the Database** -- Perform a full backup of the production database. Any time you make significant changes to a system, taking a backup is a wise choice.
- **Execute postupgrade_fixups.sql** -- DBUA runs this script as part of completing the upgrade process. This script generates three categories of information for an upgraded database: general warnings, errors, and informational recommendations. Run this script any time after completing an upgrade with DBUA or manually. Set the system to spool results to a log file so you can read the output.
- **Gather Fixed Objects Statistics** -- A few days after performing the upgrade, you should gather fixed objects statistics with the DBMS_STATS.GATHER_FIXED_OBJECTS_STATS procedure. This can have a positive impact on overall database performance.
- **Reset Passwords to Enforce Case-Sensitivity** -- Since Oracle 11g it has been possible for accounts to use case-sensitive passwords. To take advantage of enforced case-sensitive passwords for releases earlier than 11.1.0.7, you must reset the passwords of existing users during the database upgrade procedure. Executing the DBMS_VERIFIER.EXPIRE_ACCOUNTS_WITHOUT_LATEST_VERIFIER procedure will force users whose accounts do not yet have the latest verifier to change their passwords the next time they log in. For SYSDBA and SYSOPER users, you can generate a new ORAPWD file using the new command line switch ignorecase.
- **Set Threshold Values for Tablespace Alerts** -- A legacy database that has been upgraded to 12c has the Tablespace Alerts disabled. Tablespaces in the database that are candidates for monitoring should be identified and the appropriate threshold values set.

- **Migrate From Rollback Segments to Automatic Undo Mode** -- If the original database was earlier than 11g, in order to take advantage of Automatic Undo, you must migrate the database from using rollback segments to automatic undo management.
- **Migrate Tables from LONG to LOB** -- The LOB data types (BFILE, BLOB, CLOB, and NCLOB) provide multiple advantages over LONG data types. The ALTER TABLE statement can be used to change the data type of a LONG column to CLOB and that of a LONG RAW column to BLOB.

# Migrating Data by Using Oracle Data Pump

## Migrate data by using Oracle Data Pump

After you create a new empty 12c database, it is possible to use Oracle Data Pump full-mode export and import operation to move the data from your legacy database into it. The export/import operation can be performed with or without the transportable option. When this option is used on a full mode export or import, it is referred to as a full transportable export/import.

When a full transportable export/import is performed, both transportable tablespace data movement and conventional data movement are performed. Convention data movement is performed only for tables that reside in non-transportable tablespaces such as SYSTEM and SYSAUX. Both export time and import time are reduced when using a full transportable export/import.

There are some considerations when using Data Pump to move data into an Oracle 12c database:

- It is possible to import full database exports from Oracle Database 11.2.0.2 and earlier into Oracle Database 12c. However, Oracle recommends that the source database be upgraded to Oracle Database 11g release 2 (11.2.0.3 or later) so that information about registered options and components is included in the export.
- When migrating Oracle Database 11g release 2 (11.2.0.3 or later) into a 12c database using either full database export or full transportable database export, the Data Pump Export parameter VERSION=12 must be set. This will generate a dump file that is ready for import into Oracle Database 12c. If VERSION=12 is not set, the dump file will not contain complete information about registered database options and components.

- Network-based full transportable imports require use of the FULL=YES, TRANSPORTABLE=ALWAYS, and TRANSPORT_DATAFILES=datafile_name parameters. When the source database is Oracle Database 11g release 11.2.0.3 or later, but earlier than Oracle Database 12c Release 1 (12.1), the VERSION=12 parameter is also required.
- File-based full transportable imports only require use of the TRANSPORT_DATAFILES=datafile_name parameter.
- The default Data Pump directory object, DATA_PUMP_DIR, does not work with PDBs. You must define an explicit directory object within the PDB that you are exporting or importing.

# ABOUT THE AUTHOR

Matthew Morris is an Oracle Database Administrator and Developer currently employed as a Database Engineer with Computer Sciences Corporation. Matthew has worked with the Oracle database since 1996 when he worked in the RDBMS support team for Oracle Support Services. Employed with Oracle for over eleven years in support and development positions, Matthew was an early adopter of the Oracle Certified Professional program. He was one of the first one hundred Oracle Certified Database Administrators (version 7.3) and in the first hundred to become an Oracle Certified Forms Developer. In the years since, he has upgraded his Database Administrator certification for releases 8i, 9i, 10G and 11G, become an Oracle Advanced PL/SQL Developer Certified Professional and added the Expert certifications for Application Express, SQL, and SQL Tuning.

Printed in Great Britain
by Amazon.co.uk, Ltd.,
Marston Gate.